What to [Do]
with What
You've Got

The Practical Guide
to Money Management
in Retirement

Peter Weaver
Annette Buchanan

An AARP Book
published by
American Association of Retired Persons
Washington, D.C.
Scott, Foresman and Company
Lifelong Learning Division
Glenview, Illinois

Library of Congress Cataloging in Publication Data

Weaver, Peter, 1925–
        What to Do with What You've Got.

        Includes bibliographies and index.
        1. Finance, Personal. 2. Aged–Finance, Personal.
3. Retirement income. I. Buchanan, Annette, 1933–
II. Title.
HG179.W38 1984   332.024′0696   83–16505

ISBN 0–673–24805–4

Contents

About the Authors

Peter Weaver's syndicated columns on personal finance, "Mind Your Money" and "Your Retirement Dollar," are carried by such major American newspapers as *The Los Angeles Times, St. Louis Post-Dispatch,* and *The Washington Post.* He also appears on television regularly as a financial reporter and commentator for "Take Two," the midday magazine of the Cable News Network (CNN).

Weaver has served as Washington bureau chief for *Forbes* magazine and as a writer, editor, and foreign bureau chief for *Business Week.* He is the author of *You, Inc.,* about "how not to work for somebody else all your life," and *Strategies for the Second Half of Life,* about anticipating and planning for retirement while still middle-aged. He lives and writes in Bethesda, Maryland, a suburb of the nation's capital.

Annette Buchanan is an education specialist with AARP's Institute of Lifetime Learning. She previously served as coordinator of Santa Rosa Junior College's Consumer Outreach Program in Sonoma County, California. Through this program, consumer information was provided in classes and on radio and television programs. One popular course given at a senior center addressed the special concerns of older people.

As manager of the Marin and Sonoma County Offices of Consumer Credit Counselors, Buchanan helped people with financial problems focus on their spending habits and assisted them in developing a workable budget. A graduate of San Francisco State and Oregon State Universities, she now lives in Washington, D.C.

Preface

Writing this book about what to do with what you've got in retirement was a natural next step for me. A couple of years ago I wrote a book called *Strategies for the Second Half of Life* that was aimed at people in their forties and fifties.

The main strategy outlined in *Strategies* was this: The more you get your financial, physical, and emotional houses in order *before* you retire, the better off you'll be in retirement. After you retire, there often are limitations on your control over finances. This is it. You're retired.

Well, now I'm pushing 60 and this whole subject is much more important to me personally than it was before. I'm really involved in what I'm writing about. I'm worried about having enough money to be able to slow down and do some of the things I've put off all these years—travel, take some university courses.

I had always planned on being married to my first wife, Vida, during this stage of my life. She and I were a team. But things don't always work out the way you write the script. Vida died after a tough fight with cancer. My two boys had moved out on their own and, suddenly, there I was—alone.

I became involved in my wife's will, her estate (I was the executor), and all that goes with the aftermath of death. Our house was designed for a family of four or five. Now there was a family of one. Me. Right off, I thought I ought to sell the house. The maintenance costs were too much for one person. But my office was in my home, and that made it complicated. In a sense, I'd have to make two moves: one to a new residence and another to a new office space.

I started going through the whole real estate upheaval—agents asking questions, people coming by to inspect. And I was having the devil of a time finding a decent place for myself to live. I didn't know what I really wanted.

During this turmoil, I starting talking to a friend whom Vida and I had met in a local church group. Friend Kathleen was divorced and unattached. One thing led to another as we shared our feelings and we ended up keeping company.

Suddenly, my plans had to be changed again. Now, I had to look for a place for three people (Kathleen has a 14-year-old son). We couldn't find anything we wanted and after a few months I took my house off the market. We decided to live in it as a small family for the next four or five years—until my stepson is in college.

Because my bride is 17 years younger than I, after we were married we had to think about the possibility of her having to be financially independent at some time in the future. My life insurance became much more important. We had to review our finances, change titles to things, and rearrange all our credit and bank accounts.

Then, we began to dream up some long-term goals. Where did we—this new couple—want to be five years from now? What did we want to do? We thought we'd like to be in a warmer climate but not too far away from our families, friends, and roots. Maybe, we thought, we could live summers here, winters there.

I don't plan on ever retiring 100 percent. I have my own journalism and communications business, so I have some control over what I do and when I do it. I'd like to continue writing for pay—but at a slower pace as I grow older. I'm in the process of revising my investments and work projects so I will be financially able to follow the "active work/slower pace" plan.

So, you see, I really am involved personally with a lot of the issues discussed in this book—which helped a great deal during the writing process. My background in business and finance (*Business Week, Forbes* magazine, and currently a nationally syndicated personal finance column) put me in good stead, of course. I had a long list of sources and resources to draw upon.

I also got a lot of help from Alexandra Armstrong, a certified financial planner who has her own consulting firm, and from Gene Fisher, a CPA, lawyer, former IRS agent, and currently, senior partner of Aronson, Greene, Fisher & Co., accounting firm. These financial pros provided information and helped check out the authenticity of information from other sources. I benefited from our relationship in two ways. First, I got good, solid information for the book. Second, I got vital information for my own financial planning.

This can be one of the most interesting, challenging, and exciting stages of our lives—our later years—if we can get our financial underpinnings in order. This book is designed to help you do better with what you've got, so you can act out some of those dreams we all have about taking time to enjoy life.

Peter Weaver

Two people played very important roles in inspiring me to work on this book. One of these people was Tom Nelson, who directs AARP's consumer and health programs. Tom was my first supervisor at AARP. He encouraged, cajoled, questioned, and in a very positive manner supported my efforts on the book.

The other inspiration was my mother, who lived to be 90 years old. Her story illustrates what this book is all about: the importance of learning how to best manage all your financial resources for the rest of your life.

A well-educated, thoughtful, and prudent woman, my

mother prided herself on her accomplishments and abilities and never dreamed that one day she would have to rely on her children for financial support. She seemed infallible. She was left a widow with two young children and no financial resources other than a job. Living simply on a very modest income, she not only put her children through school, but she also managed to put some money aside for her retirement years.

At the age of 65 she ended her career with a state pension of less than $200 per month. To supplement this she took a part-time job for five more years. The significance of this job was that it qualified her for Social Security benefits, which she previously had not been eligible to receive. When she finally retired at age 70 she had a small monthly income and a modest savings account, and she jointly owned her home with her sister. It seemed as though she had planned well and that her retirement was secure.

My mother did not take into account what inflation and health-care costs would amount to in the remaining twenty years of her life. While the cost of living was escalating in leaps and bounds, she kept all of her savings in an account which earned so little interest that it was impossible for this "nest egg" to generate enough money to keep her savings even with the inflation rate.

Maintenance on her home was expensive, and major repairs were put off, so that when poor health and other circumstances required the sale of the home, the banks were reluctant to grant loans to potential buyers. Her last great asset was sold for a song!

The remaining years of her life were spent in ill health. Confusion with health insurance policies, hospitalization, and home health care costs quickly ate up all remaining assets. To her chagrin she had to rely on her children's support during her last years.

My hope is that this book will help *you* to do better

with what you've got so that you will have a secure and financially comfortable retirement.

Many people advised me and reviewed and critiqued my work on this book all along the way. AARP staffers who lent their expertise included Leo Baldwin, on housing; Bill Canup, on taxes; Lauri Fiori, on Social Security; Ron Hagen, on insurance; Bill McMorran and Barbara Quaintance, on health care; and DaCosta Mason, on estate planning. Banker Dan Buser, consumer protection attorney Nancy Chasen, stockbroker Girsselle Cohen, financial planner David Dondero, and real estate broker Peter Miller also provided expert commentary. My thanks to all.

I'd also like to thank Caroline Longeway and Robin Lawson and AARP's resource center staff, who provided invaluable research assistance, and Kathy Wooten, Tilly Marino, Linda Mayo, and Shirley Morris, who all helped with typing.

Annette Buchanan

This book is an educational and public service project of the American Association of Retired Persons, which, with a membership of more than 15 million, is the largest association of middle-aged and older persons in the world today. Founded in 1958, AARP provides older Americans with a wide range of membership programs and services, including legislative representation at both federal and state levels. For further information about additional association activities, write to AARP, 1909 K Street, N.W., Washington, DC 20049.

1
Introduction

You're retired, or so close to it you consider yourself already there. You may be rarin' to go, ready to try anything. Or you may have mixed emotions about the whole thing. No matter. From now on you're a member of the fastest growing "minority" in America. There are some 26 million of you— aged 65 and above—who have high hopes of making these years rank among the best.

If there is a cloud on your horizon, it may be the one that so often builds up around that old retirement nemesis: Money.

Perhaps you've read the gloomy statistics about one out of every four older citizens of this country being poor or near poor. Turn those seemingly sober statistics around, though, and you find that three out of four older Americans are *not* poor, and many of them are doing very well indeed. The majority own their homes, travel a lot, and enjoy reasonably good health. Less than 5 percent of all people over 65 are confined to bed or need help to get around their homes. That's not bad—not bad at all.

If you've made it this far, that's quite an accomplishment. And you're in good company. More and more older Americans are living longer and—compared to the past— living better. According to the U.S. Public Health Service, life expectancy for men back in the early 1940s was only 60 years. For women it was 65. Now, life expectancy for men is around 70 years and for women it's pushing 80. Apparently, the older you get the more your own life expectancy estimate tends to stretch out. For example, when you reach 65, you can reasonably expect to live to 80 and above, especially if you're a woman.

As you've seen, women in this country tend to outlive men. And this life expectancy gap (now around 8 years) keeps on getting wider.

The fact that people are living longer today, salubrious as it sounds, does present some problems. Because many retirement incomes are not keeping up with inflation, the longer one lives, the less money one tends to have. With women living longer than men, they're the ones most likely to face a paucity of funds in their later years.

Will you outlive your capital?

This potential problem of outliving your capital will be the major retirement issue you'll be facing. But don't despair. You've probably got a fair amount of capital right now or you wouldn't be reading this book, which is aimed directly at the middle-income crowd—not the poor, not the rich. You may feel that you don't have all that much money on your side of the planning table. Look around. If you own a home, chances are most of it is paid for. This means you might well have a lot of money tied up in your homestead—money that could be converted to cash. If you rent your place, you may have stashed away a tidy sum in savings or securities or both.

On top of this, you may have Social Security retirement checks, which should tend to move up with inflation and be pretty much tax free over the years. Under a new law effective in 1984, though, you'll have to pay a tax on Social Security benefits if your total annual income surpasses $25,000 ($32,000 for married couples). "Total income" includes adjusted gross income, any money from tax-exempt bonds, and one-half of your Social Security benefits.

Also, cost-of-living adjustments will be based on wages or prices, whichever are lower, if the system's trust fund balance dips below a specific level. Adjustments were formerly based on prices.

Nevertheless, your Social Security income should remain strong and steady for years to come. Politicians would be lynched if they let Social Security fall on its face. The growing multitude of older Americans has too much clout to let that happen.

If you're lucky, and a good many of you reading this book probably are, you'll have a pension or profit-sharing funds to draw on. Unfortunately, most private pension income, while nice to have, pays a fixed rate of return and can't be counted on to keep up with inflation as you grow older. And, as you've seen, there's a good chance you'll live another fifteen, twenty years or longer. So, as the years roll by, you probably will need more money. Whether you satisfy this need, or not, will depend on how cleverly you manage the capital and income potential you already have. This is precisely why this book addresses the critical question: What to Do with What You've Got.

Rule of 72

For cash planning purposes, to account for inflation, economists like to use the "Rule of 72." Although it's not perfect because of all the variables, it can serve as an indicator of how much money you'll need in future years.

Here's how it works. Pick out a rate of inflation you think will be predominant in the eighties and early nineties. As an example, take 6 percent (which some economists feel is reasonable). When you divide 72 by 6, you get 12. This means you must double your income within 12 years in order to stay even. It will take twice as many dollars to buy the basics and the lifestyle niceties you're enjoying now.

How will you find the money?
Step by step, this book will cover the income and outflow money lines on your personal balance sheet. Questions will be raised and, for the most part, answered.

Can you increase your income?
What kind of income do you have now? Can it be increased? You'll be pleasantly surprised at the methods some retirees have used to greatly increase their current incomes.

Then there's your capital—your estate. Can you squeeze income out of your major assets? The big area, of course, is home ownership. You may have a golden opportunity to convert your home into an income producer instead of an income loser.

Because money tied up in a home during retirement is so important an item on your profit and loss statement, a large portion of this book is dedicated to the subject. Read Chapters 4, 5, and 6 carefully. If they don't pertain to your needs now, chances are they will require your attention later on.

After probing your home ownership situation, you'll be taking a hard look at your other investments. These might include savings accounts, securities, life insurance (if it has cash value), and other potential income producers.

Finally, on the income side of your ledger, don't overlook your own productive powers. The human mind and body can be an amazing production machine if it's properly equipped and happily aimed in the right direction.

At this stage of the game, there are usually two types of reactions to the word *work*. If you've labored long and hard at a dull job, your reaction might well be "Ugh!" If, on the other hand, you've been happy at your toils, you might find the prospect of some gainful employment "Quite interesting."

The idea is to get paid for what you like to do, taking advantage of old skills and your current image of reliability and responsibility. Being willing and able to work part time at something you like can be a big plus on the income side of your retirement account. This could allow most, if not all, of your capital to expand, with compounding interest and dividends, so that it might be better used later on.

Consider work as a potential capital-preservation device. Work in retirement may not be for you, but don't knock it until you've given the chapter "How about working?" some careful thought.

Up to now, we've been talking about the supply side of the retirement balance sheet: your income and your capital (which might be converted into income). What about the demand side? This covers your demand for money—your needs and your desires for goods and services.

Can you decrease your demands?
If you can increase your supply of money, you also may be able to simultaneously or alternatively decrease your demand for it. Later chapters are concerned with areas where you could cut some costs without disrupting your retirement plans.

A major item that many people in retirement tend to overlook as a possible area for cost cutting is their health. If you're sick or run down, it costs money to get back into shape or to be maintained where you won't get worse.

When you reach 65, Medicare takes over some of the major medical costs. This is a real blessing. But, as you may already realize, Medicare only pays around 40 percent of your overall medical bills. The part that's not covered has been dubbed "medigap," and it's getting bigger all the time as hospital costs and doctor's bills continue to soar.

If you can find ways of taking better care of your mind and your body, you may very well be able to reduce your "medigap" costs to the minimum. Some retirees have done wonders improving their overall health outlook. You'll be getting some suggestions on how to draw up your own money-saving physical and psychological checklist.

There are other places, too, where you may be able to cut costs without cutting your enjoyment of life: your car, travel, entertainment, food, clothing, utility bills, taxes.

Set up your retirement game plan

In short, this book will show you, chapter by chapter, how to set up short-term and long-term game plans for retirement. You may not become a financial expert, but you'll learn how to have much more control over your finances. You'll also learn how to seek out and evaluate the advice of key professionals (lawyer, accountant, insurance agent, real estate agent, banker, broker).

You can get valuable assistance from most, if not all, of these pros. However, you owe it to yourself to assume as much responsibility for your financial well-being as possible. This is particularly true if you are a woman. Retired single working women, in general, have lower retirement incomes and fewer benefits than men and thus have a more difficult task in financing their retirement years. Many married women tend to let their husbands handle "all that financial stuff." Since four women out of five will survive their husbands—and live on as widows for many years—learning money management skills is of crucial importance for all older married women.

This book should serve you well as a "sideline coach" for your overall retirement strategy. If you aren't careful, you might choose one of the unpleasant extremes in financial planning. You might dig deep into your capital reserves now so you can live it up while you're still young enough to enjoy it—and outlive your capital. Or, you may scrimp too much now and never get a chance to really enjoy your hard-earned savings.

To chart a smooth course between these financial shoals, you've got to come up with some creative, sensible goals. What do you want to do and where do you want to be five years from now? ten years from now?

Once you've laid out your needs and desires for the future, you can begin the task of sorting out your personal finances to see if you can afford your dreams. Maybe you'll need quite a bit of money. Maybe not. The next chapter, "Your goals," is designed to provide ideas, insights, and guidelines on what it's going to take to make you happy in retirement—and keep you that way.

2
Your goals

To make a financial plan for the future, you have to know what that future might be like. You have to know where you want to live, how you want to live, and what kind of people you want to be near. You need to know what you want to do so far as developing your mind and your body is concerned. You may want to brush up current skills or learn new ones, and you may want to find some kind of interesting work—albeit on your own scaled-down schedule.

Put your goals on paper

All this might seem a bit confusing at this stage. If it does, you can make it less so by writing down a list of goals— things you want to accomplish this year and on out to your exit from earth. (You can use Worksheets 1 and 2 at the end of this chapter.)

Don't worry about trying to set your future in concrete. "Goals," says life- and career-planning expert John Crystal in his and Richard Bolles' excellent workbook, *Where Do I Go from Here with My Life?*, "can always be adapted, changed, or completely discarded as time goes on." A list of goals is "only a statement of how you see the future now at this moment."

So scribble away and enjoy yourself. If you're single and living alone, you probably need to plan just for yourself. If you're married or otherwise living with another person, you should both put down your individual goals. They might mesh together nicely, or quite possibly (if you're both honest), they might clash. When two people are involved, setting up goals often takes some compromising, with a good deal of love and sensitivity worked into the process.

An example of a compromise might go like this:

He—Wants to be near golf courses. Wants to fish and develop swimming and art skills in sunny Florida.

She—Wants to be near their children and grandchildren who live in Los Angeles. Also wants to continue her education in the field of literature and writing.

Solution—With help from their children and friends, they discovered the San Diego area. Many, many golf courses. Lots of sun. Good fishing. Excellent art possibilities. Near the kids and grandchildren. And first-rate university and community college courses in literature and writing.

Obviously, most compromises are more difficult to come by than this one. But, with partners willing to take a step toward the middle, some amazing compromises have been reached. More often than not, the solution turns out to be better for both than either of their individual plans.

When you retire, a whole new world of possibilities opens up. You no longer have to be at a certain spot at a certain time, with an employer (or customers) always calling the shots. Now, you have more time for yourself. The question is: How and where are you going to spend that time?

For some people, the answer is easy. They know just where they want to be right now and X years from now. For them, a doff of the hat. If you are one of these people, you can move on to the next chapter if you wish. But be careful. Even if you know what you want to do, you may not understand all the contingencies—all the twists and turns—that may occur along the way.

For most of us, retirement may cause some interim planning problems. We're not sure what we want to do—or where we want to do it. We've dabbled with dreams, but life kept moving on too quickly to be able to investigate all the possibilities.

Focus on your dreams

Whether you're single or married, you have to concentrate on your own needs and desires. Put those dreams out on the table and take a good look at them. Don't let your friends or children talk you out of what you really want to do.

For example, you may find that the idea of selling the old family home is more traumatic for your grown children than it is for you. They want to be able to come home, touch base, whenever they want. They like the continuity. But you'd just as soon move to something smaller, easier to manage, and less costly to maintain.

If you are planning for just yourself, it may be simpler in some ways than planning as a couple. You don't have to compromise to satisfy a partner's desires. You can sit down and draw up your own game plan—goal by goal.

On the other hand, you won't have someone else to bounce ideas off. Planning can be lonely, and you might overlook important aspects of your deeper needs. It's not a bad idea to have a good friend work with you on goal planning. Your dreams and schemes can get some good critical comment. Be careful whom you choose. Some friends may throw cold water on your plans because they're jealous of your new-found freedom or because they want you to stick around to keep them company.

Write goal-planning questions

With or without someone else working alongside, you have to start someplace. As a beginning, try writing down a series of goal-planning questions. Then answer them. The following questions are patterned after the kinds of questions suggested by John Crystal. Obviously, these are just a guide. You no doubt will raise other questions that should be added to this checklist.

1. Where do you want to live? This is, perhaps, the most important question of all. Do you want to remain in your current home? Or do you want to move to another part of the country? Be honest with yourself. Let your deepest dreams come forth. Crystal suggests asking this complementary question: If you had a free choice, if there were no financial restraints, where would you want to be? Give yourself two or three choices in case one is too expensive or otherwise impossible. List reasons for your choices, such as security (law and order), job opportunities, climate, activities, nearness to family and friends, clean air. (Chapters 4, 5, and 6 will help you evaluate the whole stay put or move situation.)

2. What kind of people do you want to be with? This, too, is a vital question. If you stay put, it may cost more to keep the too-large, too-cold, too-whatever place going. But, if you move out of the area, it may cost even more to build up a new "social network" of friends, professionals, and other relationships.

If you do decide to move, take time to investigate your chosen spot thoroughly. Maybe you can vacation there for a while. Find out what's what with local services, doctors, taxes, costs, and conveniences. If it's a vacation-type place, be sure you know what it's like in the off-season. What are the people like? Do you have friends there?

3. How close do you want to be to your children, brothers, sisters, or other members of your family? If you move to be near them, will you have to give up too much? Is there a compromise? Do you want to keep your current home just because the children like to visit? Would they visit some other place just as well?

4. What kind of activities do you want? Are they available where you are, or are they better someplace else?

5. Is working part time important? If so, what's the employment outlook where you are now and where you might

want to go? Check Chapter 12 for ideas on how to evaluate
employment possibilities.

**6. *How and where do you want to develop your skills and
knowledge?*** Some communities have excellent programs for
older students. Does yours? Does the place you want to move
to have nearby education opportunities?

7. *What do you want to accomplish before you die?* Do you
want to win a senior tennis tournament? Do you want to
write a book about your life—for your family, if for no one
else? Do you want to make a pilgrimage to trace your family
roots? Do you want to travel the globe? Build a boat? What?
These are the questions dreams are made of. And, dreams
can come true. Listen to what John Crystal says:

". . . ignore the lifelong brainwashing our culture has
given each of us, that we should not visualize what we most
like to do because it will be impossible to achieve it anyway.
You should spell out your impossible dreams to translate
them into alternative ways and means, and to pursue vigor-
ously your whole dream with your whole heart."

Dream the impossible dream—that's what the Man
from La Mancha implored us to do in the musical's theme
song. But dreams have a better chance of coming true if
we put them down on paper and work them into the real
world.

Play contingency games

To make sure your dreams have a chance of materializing,
and to insulate yourself against future disappointment or di-
saster, you should play contingency games with your listed
goals. For example, if you're married: What if your spouse
dies or becomes disabled in some far-off beach, mountain,
or desert world that seemed ever so alluring at first glance?

If you're single: Will you become isolated if a best friend succumbs? What would living alone be like? Are there other friends and family members nearby? Are there medical facilities within easy distance? Will there be enough money to cover costs of needed care if you are temporarily or permanently disabled?

If two of you are involved in goal planning, perhaps one should play the part of the devil's advocate. You have to get an idea of how your dreams might stand up to reality.

One of the biggest challenges will be having enough money to make it all happen. Unfortunately, you can't get a good grip on this slippery subject until you've toted up what you have going for you—and against you.

In the next chapter you'll become acquainted with your own personal balance sheet—what's coming in, what's going out, what you own, and what you owe.

Ready resources

The Three Boxes of Life: And How to Get Out of Them (Ten Speed Press), by Richard Bolles. This book's major theme evolves from the author's contention that we should have education, work, and leisure (the three boxes) merged together to be active in all stages of our lives. There are some good chapters on setting up goals and on finding out about yourself and what you really want to do.

Re-Engagement in Later Life: Re-Employment and Re-Marriage (Greylock Press), by Dr. Ruth Harriet Jacobs and Dr. Barbara H. Vinik. This book presents case studies of retired people who went back to work and/or remarried after being widowed or divorced. Good illustrations of how people change life plans and adjust to those changes.

Worksheet 1   Short-term goals

Briefly describe your short-term goals in the categories listed. For example, in the housing category, your goal for this year may be to "stay put." Within 5 years your goal may be to "move to condo in Sarasota."

Goal categories	This year	Within 5 years
Housing		
Hobbies		
Travel, visits (long-term)		
Volunteer work		
Education		
Employment, business		
Major purchases, auto		
Cultural, social		
Fitness, recreation		
Gifts, other		

Worksheet 2   Long-term goals

Briefly describe your long-term goals in the different categories listed. Provide contingency plans. For example, for housing, your goal may be to "stay put," but if your spouse dies, your goal may be to "live with sister."

Goal categories	Within 5–10 years	10 or more years
Housing		
Hobbies		
Travel, visits (long-term)		
Volunteer work		
Education		
Employment, business		
Major purchases, auto		
Cultural, social		
Fitness, recreation		
Gifts, other		

3
The bottom line

You've dreamed the impossible dream. You've put all your hopes and desires down on paper, along with your basic needs. Now, you've got to add up your income and assets to see where you stand. Are your dreams within reach? If not, is there something you can do about your financial situation: cut costs, add income?

Calculate your net worth

Although financial planners and accountants like to start right off with a hard-nosed balance sheet giving details of all the money coming in and going out, you can put that aside for a moment and add up your overall net worth (use Worksheet 3 at the end of this chapter for guidance).

For many retired persons, adding up their net worth can be a most pleasant experience. How much they've been able to amass over the years may come as a surprise. Their home equity value, their collection of antiques, coins, or whatever may have doubled, even tripled, in resale value. Maybe they have cash built up through their insurance policies and never realized how much was there.

List your assets

To find out how much you have, list all the things you own that have current market or resale value. Start with your home, if you're an owner. This is your most important asset.

It may be worth lots more than you think or, heaven forbid, less than you think.

You should call two or three real estate firms for estimates on your home's current, competitive, market value. They'll usually do this, no charge, because they want to line you up as a prospective client when you finally do decide to sell the place. When you get a realty firms' ballpark figure of what your home might sell for, knock the price down about 10 percent to cover the firms' tendencies to overestimate and to cover all the commissions and fees you'll have to pay when you sell.

You might want to have a professional appraiser do a thorough inspection and appraisal for a fee ($100 to $300, depending on location and estimated market value). It will be more accurate than most real estate firms' appraisals, and it can serve as an excellent marketing tool if you decide to sell. (Most lenders know good appraisers to recommend.)

After your home, your next most important assets will probably be your savings, securities, rental property, and IRA or Keogh funds. List the current value of all these items.

If you have any valuable, marketable collections, antiques, or other items that could be fairly easily turned into cash, list them too. It might not be a bad idea at this stage to have these items appraised (you can get names of appraisers from bank trust departments or local probate court officials). For insurance purposes, if for nothing else, you should know the current value of your antiques, coin collections, and the like. Inflation may have multiplied their values many times over the past ten years.

Because an insurance agent wanted a detailed replacement value figure, a retired couple was pleasantly shocked to learn that their porcelain collection (handed down over two generations) was worth more than $40,000. They had recently guessed the value at less than $8,000.

If you have a fairly new, fairly expensive car, boat, or other such marketable possession, put down the fair market value—what could you really sell it for? Newspaper and magazine classifieds and dealers can be a help with this.

Perhaps you have an insurance policy or policies that have piled up cash value. Find out from your insurer what the cash-in value is and jot it down (that'll stir'em up, but more on this in Chapter 10).

List your liabilities

After basking in the glow of your new-found wealth, swing your pencil over to the minus side of the ledger and start jotting down all the money you owe. How much is left on your home mortgage(s)? Do you have a second mortgage? How about that car or boat loan? Any money owed on revolving credit accounts with stores or to plastic card issuers?

Add up both columns now—assets and liabilities—and subtract the latter total from the former. This will give you a quick snapshot of your so-called net worth.

You may want to differentiate between liquid and non-liquid assets and between fixed and variable liabilities. Liquid assets are easy to convert to cash—perhaps with just a phone call. With non-liquid assets, it would take some time to determine the value and make a sale. Fixed liabilities are set in time (your mortgage, for example), while variable liabilities change over time.

Figure annual income and expenses

After you've nailed down your net worth, you should move on to your weekly, monthly, and annual income and cost-of-operation figures—cash in, cash out.

List income sources

Social Security retirement benefit checks probably are a major cash-in item. For many retired people, Social Security provides at least half the monthly income. If not Social Security, you might have Civil Service, military, railroad, or other such retirement benefits coming from the government.

If, for any reason, you think there's something really wrong with your current Social Security income figure, check your master record of earnings credited to your Social Security account. Your benefits are based on this master record. Ask your nearest Social Security office for the postcard "Request for Statement of Earnings." Fill out this preaddressed card and send it to Social Security headquarters in Baltimore. You'll receive a statement of earnings.

Check the statement against your records of past wages (from your employers' W-2 forms). If there is a discrepancy, call your local Social Security office. Officials in your area are usually good at helping you sort things out. If not, ask for the address of the Baltimore headquarters' complaint and referral center (it changes from time to time).

If you haven't retired yet, you should check your master record at least a year before you retire. This gives you time to possibly correct the record before you apply for benefits (which you should do about four months before you retire).

If you are divorced, it is important that you know that divorced spouses (married at least ten years) can now draw benefits at age 62 if their former spouses are *eligible* for benefits. Previously, the former spouse had to be actually *receiving* benefits.

Presuming your Social Security benefits are okay, you can move on and list your private pension benefits (if you're lucky enough to have them). Money coming from annuities, trusts, and the like should also be penciled in.

This is your "fixed" income. You get it no matter what happens (a big advantage over wage earners who can get cut off in a recession). Next, put down your sources of variable income. These should include such things as savings interest, dividends, part-time job wages, and rental income. But don't list any income you're not actually taking out and using. If it's plowed back into increasing your savings or securities accounts (or put into refurbishing your rental property), don't count it as income—it's part of your assets, your capital base.

If you have a little home business that makes money, list this income too. You might have to estimate what it might be on an annual basis.

List costs

Income sources are pretty easy to locate and put to paper. Costs are another matter. There are many more of them and some are elusive. To get a good picture of your cost of living, fill in what accountant and lecturer Paul Offenbacher calls a "financial calendar."

For each month put down all your fixed costs (e.g., mortgage, $200; pro rata property taxes, $230; pro rata insurance premiums, $180). Anything that must be paid regularly, no matter what, should go in here. You can prorate insurance and tax items for each month or put them down, lump sum, in the months when they're due—whichever is more convenient.

To get an idea of your variable costs (food, clothing, transportation, utilities, repairs, maintenance, entertainment) go back over your checkbook entries during the past three or four months and dig out some averages. Add or subtract dollar amounts according to what you think the next twelve months will be like (more, or less, heating or air conditioning, big clothing items coming up).

When you've added up all your variable expenses (use Worksheet 4 at the end of the chapter to make things easier), you can merge them with your fixed costs to see how much money goes out every month and how much goes out on an annual basis.

You might like to compare your annual budget allocations to those of an "average" retired couple according to the last (1981) statistics from the U.S. Bureau of Labor: housing, 33%; food, 29%; medical care, 10%; transportation,

10%; clothing and personal care, 7%; gifts and contributions, 6%; and recreation, education, other, 5%.

How's your cash flow?

So, now you have it. Money in, money out. Hopefully, you will have a surplus at the end of the year. This is called a positive cash flow and it's certainly nice to have. If you have a negative cash flow, more money going out than coming in, you've got some real work to do, quick (unless there was something exceptional, such as a pile of unreimbursed medical bills). Some of the ways to turn a negative cash flow into something more positive in retirement are to chop expenses, to convert some assets to income, to get a part-time job, and to tune up your investments.

Assuming your cash-flow test is positive, you might want to "pay yourself" at the end of the year. Accountant Paul Offenbacher says it's not mandatory in retirement, "but it's a healthy goal you should consider." Here's how it works:

Let's say your retirement income is $15,000 a year. And your total cash-out costs for the year come to $13,000. This gives you a $2,000 surplus. Instead of using up all of the surplus for trips, major purchases, and the like, Offenbacher suggests plowing 10 percent of your income figure back into savings and investments—paying yourself. (This percentage may be a bit high for you, but see what you can do.)

Ten percent of $15,000 comes to $1,500. You subtract this from your $2,000 surplus and you have $500 left over. Not much, you say, for fun and games. True. "Maybe you can take on an interesting part-time job," says Offenbacher, "to boost the $500 up to $2,000 or more." In effect, your job money becomes a major addition to your $500 "mad money."

With this little, somewhat simplistic, example, you can see how one can pay for the necessities of life, keep one's capital intact, and *still* have enough left over to invest in those dreams you wrote down in Chapter 2.

For some retirees, there will be more dream money at the end of the year. For others, there will be precious little. If you're one of the latter, perhaps you can find money elsewhere. Getting a job has been mentioned. Starting up your own little business is a possibility (more on all this in Chapter 12).

You might be able to convert your home into an income producer instead of an income loser (this will be covered in Chapter 4). Or, moving to a smaller place near shopping and other activities might cut your monthly mortgage or rental fee, utility bills, and transportation costs—not to mention your taxes, insurance, and upkeep costs. You might be able to sell your car (a major cost item) and use taxis, buses, your feet, and occasional rental cars.

So, you see, your cash flow sheet is more than a profit and loss statement. It's a potential checklist for soft spots where money can be saved and assets can be converted into cash.

Project your budget into the future

So far as the long haul is concerned, you can project your cash-in, cash-out budget for a year or so. After that, things become iffy. There are so many variables. Will Social Security continue to provide some sort of cost-of-living allowance? If so, how much? What about unreimbursed medical costs— what will they be? What will happen to interest rates and property taxes?

For long-range planning, you can use Table 1 at the end of the chapter to help you project how current costs will grow with compounded inflation yearly. But keep in mind that long-range projections can give you just a rough idea of what your actual budget will be.

To help with your long-haul planning and budget projections, you might want to subscribe to one of the computerized financial planning services. You fill in a detailed questionnaire that covers all the items on your personal balance sheet. And you answer a number of questions about your personal goals and desires. An inflation factor (currently ranging from 5 to 7 percent) is cranked in and you get a weighted projection of how much you'll need over the years and where it might come from.

If you're interested in getting some outside help on your budget projections, you might try one of these services. Be sure that the service has special questionnaires and printouts for retired people, whose needs differ from those of pre-retirees. One service that does is the Institute of Financial Management, Ltd., 2100 M Street, N.W., Washington, DC 20063. The cost: $45.

Ready resources

Pension Rights Center, 1436 Connecticut Avenue, N.W., Room 1019, Washington, DC 20036. This organization publishes a valuable bulletin called **Pension Facts** (with a special section for women). It spells out your rights to private pensions and is particularly good at alerting people about changes in government and private pension rulings (such as new pension rights for divorced military wives, foreign service wives, and others).

American Council on Life Insurance, 1850 K Street, N.W., Washington, DC 20006. This organization offers help to retirees (especially widows) who believe they have insurance money coming but don't know the name of the insurer or how to find it.

Make your Money Grow (Dell Books). This easy-to-read primer on budgeting, saving, and investing is written by the editors of **Changing Times** magazine.

Worksheet 3   Net worth statement

List the current dollar value of assets owned by you, your spouse, jointly, or in common.

	You	Spouse	Joint	Common
Assets **(current value)**				
Checking acct. bal.	$_____	$_____	$_____	$_____
Savings acct. bal.	_____	_____	_____	_____
Cash in safe deposit box, safe, cash box	_____	_____	_____	_____
U.S. gov't securities	_____	_____	_____	_____
U.S. savings bonds	_____	_____	_____	_____
Certificates of deposit	_____	_____	_____	_____
Money market fund	_____	_____	_____	_____
Insurance cash value	_____	_____	_____	_____
IRA, Keogh, pension, annuities (total payable to survivors)	_____	_____	_____	_____
Stocks	_____	_____	_____	_____
Bonds	_____	_____	_____	_____
Mutual fund	_____	_____	_____	_____
Estimated value of residence(s)	_____	_____	_____	_____
Other real estate	_____	_____	_____	_____
Debts owed to you	_____	_____	_____	_____
Automobile(s)and other vehicles	_____	_____	_____	_____
Appliances, tools, equipment	_____	_____	_____	_____
Furniture (resale)	_____	_____	_____	_____
Jewelry	_____	_____	_____	_____
Collectibles	_____	_____	_____	_____
Business share(s)	_____	_____	_____	_____
Totals	$_____	$_____	$_____	$_____

Worksheet 3   Net worth statement

	You	Spouse	Joint	Common
Liabilities (exclude normal expenses such as food and rent)				
Bills payable	$_____	$_____	$_____	$_____
Home mortgage bal.	_____	_____	_____	_____
Balance on other real estate mortgage	_____	_____	_____	_____
Balance on loans, installment contracts	_____	_____	_____	_____
Estimated income and real estate taxes payable this year	_____	_____	_____	_____
Pledges to charities	_____	_____	_____	_____
Gifts promised	_____	_____	_____	_____
Other	_____	_____	_____	_____
Totals	$_____	$_____	$_____	$_____

Find your net worth

List your total assets $ _____
Subtract total liabilities   −$ _____
Your net worth   =$ _____

Worksheet 4   Income and expenses

List fixed and variable income for each month and total down to arrive at total monthly income. Add across to find years totals. Do the same for expenses.

	Jan	Feb	Mar	Apr	May	June
Fixed income						
Social Security	$ ___	___	___	___	___	___
Pension, annuity	___	___	___	___	___	___
Wages	___	___	___	___	___	___
Rent	___	___	___	___	___	___
Other	___	___	___	___	___	___
Variable income						
Interest	$ ___	___	___	___	___	___
Dividends	___	___	___	___	___	___
Other	___	___	___	___	___	___
Total income	$ ___	___	___	___	___	___
Fixed expenses						
Rent, mortgage	$ ___	___	___	___	___	___
Property taxes	___	___	___	___	___	___
Insurance	___	___	___	___	___	___
Loan payments	___	___	___	___	___	___
Other	___	___	___	___	___	___
Variable expenses						
Maintenance	$ ___	___	___	___	___	___
Utilities, services	___	___	___	___	___	___
Auto upkeep	___	___	___	___	___	___
Medical	___	___	___	___	___	___
Furnishings	___	___	___	___	___	___
Food, household	___	___	___	___	___	___
Clothing, personal	___	___	___	___	___	___
Education	___	___	___	___	___	___
Recreation, gifts	___	___	___	___	___	___
Other	___	___	___	___	___	___
Total expenses	$ ___	___	___	___	___	___

Worksheet 4   Income and expenses

Year's
totals

July	Aug	Sept	Oct	Nov	Dec		
___	___	___	___	___	___		$___
___	___	___	___	___	___		___
___	___	___	___	___	___		___
___	___	___	___	___	___		___
___	___	___	___	___	___		___
___	___	___	___	___	___		$___
___	___	___	___	___	___		___
___	___	___	___	___	___		___
___	___	___	___	___	___	**Total income**	$___
___	___	___	___	___	___		$___
___	___	___	___	___	___		___
___	___	___	___	___	___		___
___	___	___	___	___	___		___
___	___	___	___	___	___		___
___	___	___	___	___	___		$___
___	___	___	___	___	___		___
___	___	___	___	___	___		___
___	___	___	___	___	___		___
___	___	___	___	___	___		___
___	___	___	___	___	___		___
___	___	___	___	___	___		___
___	___	___	___	___	___		___
___	___	___	___	___	___		___
___	___	___	___	___	___	**Total expenses**	$___

Table 1   Inflation multiplying factors

Choose an appropriate inflation rate—for example, 6 percent. Multiply your expenses by the factors listed in the 6 percent column to project how costs will grow and compound 1 year from now and so on.

Inflation rates

Years	5%	6%	7%	8%	9%	10%	11%	12%	13%	14%
1	1.05	1.06	1.07	1.08	1.09	1.10	1.11	1.12	1.13	1.14
2	1.10	1.12	1.14	1.16	1.18	1.21	1.23	1.25	1.27	1.29
3	1.15	1.19	1.22	1.25	1.29	1.33	1.36	1.40	1.44	1.48
4	1.21	1.26	1.31	1.36	1.41	1.46	1.51	1.57	1.63	1.68
5	1.27	1.33	1.40	1.46	1.53	1.61	1.68	1.76	1.84	1.92
6	1.34	1.41	1.50	1.58	1.67	1.77	1.87	1.97	2.08	2.19
7	1.40	1.50	1.60	1.71	1.82	1.94	2.07	2.21	2.35	2.50
8	1.47	1.59	1.71	1.85	1.99	2.14	2.30	2.47	2.65	2.85
9	1.55	1.68	1.83	1.99	2.17	2.35	2.55	2.77	3.00	3.25
10	1.62	1.79	1.96	2.15	2.36	2.59	2.83	3.10	3.39	3.70
11	1.71	1.89	2.10	2.33	2.58	2.85	3.15	3.47	3.83	4.22
12	1.79	2.01	2.25	2.51	2.81	3.13	3.49	3.89	4.33	4.81
13	1.88	2.13	2.40	2.71	3.06	3.45	3.88	4.36	4.89	5.49
14	1.97	2.26	2.57	2.93	3.34	3.79	4.31	4.88	5.53	6.26
15	2.07	2.39	2.74	3.17	3.64	4.17	4.78	5.47	6.25	7.13
16	2.18	2.54	2.95	3.42	3.97	4.59	5.31	6.13	7.06	8.13
17	2.29	2.69	3.15	3.70	4.32	5.05	5.89	6.86	7.98	9.27
18	2.40	2.85	3.37	3.99	4.71	5.55	6.54	7.68	9.02	10.57
19	2.52	3.02	3.61	4.31	5.14	6.11	7.26	8.61	10.19	12.05
20	2.65	3.20	3.86	4.66	5.60	6.72	8.06	9.64	11.52	13.74
21	2.78	3.39	4.14	5.03	6.10	7.40	8.94	10.80	13.02	15.66
22	2.92	3.60	4.43	5.43	6.65	8.14	9.93	12.10	14.71	17.86
23	3.07	3.81	4.74	5.87	7.25	8.95	11.02	13.55	16.62	20.36
24	3.22	4.04	5.07	6.34	7.91	9.84	12.23	15.17	18.78	23.21
25	3.38	4.29	5.42	6.84	8.62	10.83	13.58	17.00	21.23	26.46

4
Staying put:
pros and cons

Your home is your shelter, your base of operations. It can be your castle. Or it can be your dungeon—costing far more than necessary to heat, cool, maintain, and repair. Before you can put your financial planning into full gear, you've got to decide whether you should stick with your present abode or move to a place that costs less and better suits your current style of living. It's a big decision—one of the biggest. Stay or move?

The positive possibility

The possible advantages in staying are many and varied. You've spent a lot of time and money on the place and it suits you. You know where everything is and you're comfortable with your surroundings. Sure, there may be a few too many bedrooms, but you might be able to turn at least one of them into a den, home office (for that small business you always wanted to start), or storage catchall.

And don't forget your roots—they may be sunk down deep. Your neighborhood is friendly and familiar. Your "social network" we talked about earlier is set firmly in place. You're known at the local pharmacy, bank, repair shop—you name it. They know you and you can count on them.

Friends and relatives may live nearby. This gives you a great sense of community and security. Moving out might seriously disrupt your emotional relationships, which have been carefully and lovingly established over the years.

Your furniture (a major investment) goes well with this place. You have plenty of room for visitors, including your children, grandchildren, brothers, sisters, college chums, whomever. Your church or synagogue is nearby, as are your clubs, associations, and other groups. Perhaps you have some little business going or a part-time job you don't want to throw over by moving elsewhere.

Your mortgage may be paid off. You're getting some sort of discount on property taxes because of your age. Living here seems to fit your budget.

That's the positive possibility. If things add up right, stay where you are. You may want to move at some future date, but right now you have it made. Staying put should be your first choice if it suits your emotional make-up and, of course, your pocketbook.

The negative side

Now, let's look at the negative side. Right off, you might say you can't afford it. Although the mortgage may have been paid off (or is relatively small by today's standards), property taxes and everything else are sky high. Your utility bills are frightening and your homeowners insurance is double what it was. More and more things seem to be going wrong and need fixing (plumbing, roof—whatever).

You have far too much space. You're heating or cooling large blobs of space you don't need. You may be living in your home as a single person or as a couple and the place was originally designed to house a family of five.

Maintaining the yard, the rooms, and the like may be getting you down. Time was, you liked to do that kind of work. But not now. And getting someone else to do it for pay is too expensive.

Friends and family members may have moved to the other side of town or, more likely, to another state. Your neighborhood may have changed personality. Your surroundings may no longer be as secure as they used to be. Burglaries may be frequent.

Last but not least, the climate may be getting to you. For many retired people, winters can be downright depressing. You could take snow, sleet, and ice when you were younger. But not now. Or you might be burning up in overly long summers and want a more even climate.

The important reasons for moving, then, are escalating costs, your health, a changed neighborhood, distance from family, too much space to manage, and the climate.

If, per chance, your only hang-up about staying is cost, perhaps you haven't explored the possibility of making your home pay for itself. Many retired persons have turned their homes into income producers (or savers) instead of losers. The rest of this chapter explores some options you might have.

Renting rooms

The old boarding houses or "room-to-let" places of yore are making a comeback. Just look in any metropolitan newspaper classified section and you'll find columns filled with ads placed by amateur landlords for "professional person, nonsmoker" to rent a nice room in town or in the suburbs. Why is there a boom on for rental rooms? On the demand side, many young working people these days just cannot afford the money it takes to have their own private apartments. And older renters, too, need a good place to live at a good price. Demand is growing because the supply of apartment rental units is drying up. Existing buildings are converting to condominiums, and developers seem loath to embark on new rental projects. Meanwhile, the price for rental units keeps going up and up.

On the supply side, many a retired person has learned that there is money to be made in the room rental business. And, there are the tax advantages that go with running your own little business (depreciation allowances, deductions for heating and air conditioning, maintenance costs, and the like). There's one potential disadvantage. When you sell your home, you may have to pay additional taxes on the portion that was rented and depreciated. Check with a tax specialist on this well before you put your home on the market.

Depending on where you live, you can get from $80 a month rent for a small room on up to $400 a month for a basement apartment. Rooms are easy to open up because there's nothing to do except, perhaps, put on a fresh coat of paint or install a new bed, dresser, or whatever.

Converting your basement (attic, wing, garage) into an apartment is another matter. You may have to do a considerable amount of remodeling, which could cost thousands of dollars. But the result could be a marketable unit for current income and tax deductions.

Before you rush out to get an architect or contractor to convert part of your place into a rental unit, check your zoning laws. Chances are, you can't have a rental apartment per se. Or perhaps you can have an apartment with bedroom, living-dining area, bathroom, but no kitchen. Local laws vary. Some homeowners have gotten around zoning laws by installing a small refrigerator and hot plate unit or microwave instead of a traditional range (which may be forbidden). Most architects and contractors know the ins and outs of the zoning laws.

In some areas, zoning restrictions are being modified to give retired people the right to make rental money out of their homes. Check with your Area Agency on Aging about this. It will be listed under your county or city in your phone book, or you can get the number from your mayor's office.

On the plus side, besides the money you make, you might be able to find a first-rate tenant who can provide good company and a sense of security. You're less apt to become a burglary victim with a tenant around. And, in an emergency, there's someone there to provide assistance. In some cases, you might be able to reduce the rent in exchange for some services supplied by the tenant (yard chores, maintenance, shopping, preparing meals).

There are some possible disadvantages you should consider. One big one is the loss of privacy, particularly if you have to share a bathroom and kitchen.

Choosing the right tenant is paramount. Applicants must be thoroughly checked out and interviewed. You may want to select someone with common interests and lifestyle— e.g., nonsmoker, decent hours, neat and tidy.

Take care with how you word your newspaper ad. Read the classifieds for several weeks to see what's being emphasized. When applicants start coming by for a look-see and an interview, you've got to get references, place of work, last residence, banking, and credit sources.

Fortunately, much of this type of organization has already been done for you in an excellent book, *Living with Tenants*, written by Doreen Bierbrier, a mini-landlord who has turned renting rooms into a thriving business. The book contains checklists and forms for selecting tenants, sample contracts, and other aids for novice landlords. For information on how you can get a copy, write: The Housing Connection, Box 5536, Arlington, VA 22205.

Home sharing

Some communities have "home share" projects underway and you may be able to get help with the sharer selection process (qualified applicants who will share expenses and chores). In many instances, trained professionals and volunteers match up older homeowners who want to stay where they are, but don't have enough money, with others who need a place to stay but can't afford their own apartments.

Montgomery County, Maryland, has been very successful with a home sharing project. Hundreds of seniors who need extra income and/or help maintaining their homes have been matched up with sharers of all ages. In Sarasota, Florida, The Senior Friendship Center has been running "Project Home Share" since 1979 with considerable success.

The reason these projects, and others like them, have been so successful is that trained professionals and volunteers assist with the matchmaking. A lot of interviews, background research, and screening needs to be done to come up with the right combinations. If you do the screening on your own, take time and care. Perhaps you can get some help from someone who has been through the process.

For more information on community home sharing projects, write: Shared Housing Resource Center, Department MV, 6344 Green Street, Philadelphia, PA 19144.

Bed and breakfast

Instead of the full-time, live-in sharing arrangement, you might want to consider the "bed and breakfast" approach. A burgeoning business is evolving from the old English-European concept of "taking in travelers." You provide nice, cheery rooms (usually with bath) in a convenient location for business travelers and vacationers. As a rule, you also provide a simple breakfast (coffee, toast, and juice) plus information and advice on where to go and what to do.

According to Diana McLeish, who operates the Bed and Breakfast League, rooms for singles cost around $30 a night with breakfast. Couples pay $38. Host members of the league pay $50 a year for a listing in a catalog of B&B establishments around the United States, Canada, and Europe, plus a small fee for a billing and collection service. League members who want to be guests only pay $25 a year. For information, write: Bed and Breakfast League, 2855 29th Street, N.W., Washington, DC 20008.

Besides the Bed and Breakfast League, there's the American Bed and Breakfast Association, P.O. Box 23486,

Washington, DC 20024. This organization lists leagues, associations, and individuals around the country (including Mrs. McLeish) and provides a newsletter for members. Cost of membership is $15 for guests and $25 for hosts. For $15 extra, prospective hosts can get a "start-up kit."

There are at least 150 B&B organizations around the country, including some well-established regional hosts. Pineapple Hospitality, for example, specializes in the New England area (384 Rodney French Boulevard, New Bedford, MA 02744). Bed and Breakfast International has a few places around the country and abroad but specializes in the San Francisco Bay area (151 Ardmore Road, Kensington, CA 94707).

Convert equity into income

If you've lived in your home for a while and have paid down the mortgage or paid it off, you may have a wealth of equity (the part you own). This means you may not be paying much, if anything, on your mortgage. It also means you've probably got a lot of money tied up in your home, and it can't do you much good just sitting there. With taxes, maintenance bills, and the like piling up, you may be "house rich and cash poor." It might be nice to get your hands on some of that home equity money so you can make other use of it.

But, you say, to do that you'd have to sell the place. At the moment, you may not want to sell—for any of the number of reasons we've already discussed. There are other ways, however, to siphon off equity.

Home equity conversion plans

Several new financing schemes have been devised to help older homeowners draw on their home equity while remaining in their homes. These plans—reverse mortgages, sale-leasebacks, and deferred tax payment plans—are relatively new concepts and are not available in most communities. But they're catching on and are expected to spread rapidly as the kinks are ironed out in the pilot programs.

Reverse mortgages With a reverse mortgage a homeowner with a mortgage-free home takes out a loan to the maximum limit allowed by a lending institution—usually 60 to 80 percent of the appraised value of the property. The loan funds then are paid out to the homeowner—usually in the form of monthly payments over a specific period of time such as seven to ten years. The institution may deduct insurance and taxes from each monthly payment, or the homeowner may pay these on his or her own. The homeowner continues to pay maintenance and utilities costs.

At the end of the loan term the loan must be repaid, which may require that the homeowner sell the house. Should the homeowner die before the end of the term the loan also must be repaid, usually by sale of the house. In either case, if the house is sold, the homeowner or heirs keep any remaining profits not used to satisfy the loan debt.

To overcome the shortcomings of the reverse mortgage—the possible loss of the home and the cut-off of monthly funds—one company has developed a "shared equity" reverse mortgage. This permits the homeowner to remain in the home indefinitely and continue to receive the agreed-upon monthly payment as long as the home is occupied by the owner.

Sale-leasebacks In sale-leaseback transactions, a private investor or qualified community organization purchases a home at a price 15 percent to 30 percent lower than appraised value. A down payment of 10 percent of the purchase price is paid the seller, and the balance is paid in installments over a number of years based on the actuarial life expectancy of the seller. At the time of the sale, a lease is entered into so that the former homeowner becomes a renter. Should the renter choose to give up occupancy of the house the payments would continue. Should the renter die, payments would be made to the estate.

A potential problem with a sale leaseback is that the seller/renter might outlive the actuarially calculated payments. To avoid this problem, the seller should consider as a part of the sale agreement having the buyer pay the premium on a deferred annuity with the seller as the beneficiary. The annuity would provide for the payment of funds to the renter for as long as he or she lived, regardless of place of residence.

In sale-leaseback transactions, the buyer assumes the payment of real estate taxes, major maintenance, and insurance.

Deferred tax payment plans In a number of states, older homeowners may apply for deferment of real estate taxes until the homeowner sells the property or dies. This deferment is recorded by registering a lien on the property. The deferment is private and does not interfere with the owner's right to occupy the premises. When the property is sold, the deferred taxes plus accumulated interest charges (well below market rates) must be paid and the lien thus satisfied before the title can be cleared for transfer.

Several organizations are now studying the possibility of a similar arrangement to provide for other situations such as the payment of health-care costs or in-home long-term care.

With any of these home equity conversion plans, you get to have your cake (the home) and eat it too (use of your equity). While this sounds enticing, there can be major problems. There are tax ramifications involved, and you must fully understand the long-term and irreversible housing and financial commitments you are making. Before you commit yourself, be sure to check with a lawyer or accountant who understands the process.

Still, there are older homeowners who have done well with these plans, continuing to live in their homes with added income. Leo Baldwin, AARP Housing Coordinator, is optimistic that these plans will offer good options for many older homeowners in the future. Says Baldwin: "Their homes are the major assets of most older homeowners. We must explore ways for them to use this resource as their circumstances justify, but we must also make sure that the interests of the homeowner are protected as fully as the interests of the financial community. AARP is actively monitoring the legislation and home equity plans being developed."

For more information on the possibility of home equity conversion projects available in your area, write: The National Center for Home Equity Conversion, 110 East Main Street, Room 1010, Madison, WI 53703.

Life estate agreements

You can make another type of agreement, called a life estate contract, with any charitable organization that's set up to handle it, such as colleges and universities, major medical research organizations, and religious groups. You donate your home in exchange for a token fee and get to live in it for the rest of your life. Plans differ. Sometimes your home expenses are paid for by the institution. Sometimes you get a monthly stipend. All sorts of tax breaks—and problems— are involved. It's important to have any such charitable gift program explained thoroughly by a tax expert.

Refinancing

A much easier approach than life estate agreements or home equity conversions might be refinancing through a lender (mortgage banking company, bank, savings institution). You get a new—and bigger—mortgage on your home, pay off the old mortgage (if it's still there), and keep the extra cash. You get a loan based on your home's current appraised value, which may be (depending on how long you've owned it) several times what you paid for it.

"Refinancing," says real estate lawyer and author Benny Kass, "is not for everyone because you suddenly have much bigger monthly mortgage payments. . . . It should be carefully checked out with prospective lenders, your tax accountant, and your lawyer." If you are planning on moving after five years or so, Kass says, "refinancing now will give you money to spend and a possible tax break."

The big catch, of course, is that you're going to face much bigger monthly loan payments. But, says Kass, "you can set up a cash kitty to help pay the extra amount."

Here's how it might work. Let's say your home is currently valued at $150,000. You have $10,000 left to pay on the $50,000 mortgage (your home cost $60,000). A lender says you can take out $100,000 on a new mortgage if you want.

You pay off your old mortgage and have $90,000 left. To help handle the new monthly mortgage payments (which will be much higher than the old amount), you split off $45,000 for a safe and easy-access investment kitty. A money market account or fund should serve you well. Such investments pay relatively high interest and you can take money out any time to help pay off your new mortgage.

The remaining $45,000 can be used to cover basic living expenses plus some of those retirement dreams (travel, boat, college degree). If your home continues to appreciate in value, you can pay off the new loan when you sell, and you will still have plenty of equity left over to invest in a new place.

An added attraction to refinancing is the potential tax

break for people in higher tax brackets. The increased amount of interest you'll be paying on the new loan can be a sizable tax deduction.

Don't make a refinancing move without consulting a tax expert and a lawyer. Make sure your home is in an area where property values are expected to keep on rising and not the other way around.

Find an investor

Your home was a good investment for you and it may be a good investment for one of your children, another member of your family, or anyone else who has some investment money to spend and has a need for tax relief. A recent change in the tax laws now allows one of your children to take a full depreciation deduction if he or she buys your home at fair market value and leases it back to you. Previously, little or no depreciation deduction was allowed.

So, sons and daughters who need a tax break can now buy you out and become your landlord. You can be paid through an installment plan, which can provide a nice income. You'll have to pay your son or daughter a fair-market rent, but you'll be taking in a good bit more than you'll be paying out. A dividend: If you're over 55 and meet all the IRS requirements, the first $125,000 of the profit you make on the sale will be tax free.

You'll be getting good income from the sale and you'll continue to live in your home as before. On top of that, your child—as landlord—will be paying the bills for repairs, insurance, and property taxes. All of these items should be tax deductible for your son or daughter.

As an alternative ploy, your child's accountant should investigate the possibility of just taking income tax deductions for the interest paid on the home loan and property tax payments. This way you could live in your home rent free. By giving up the depreciation deduction (and the insurance), your son or daughter does not have to charge any rent.

Remember, this kind of a legal deal is not for everyone. It needs careful study by a lawyer and a tax adviser. You want to make sure that you will have a guaranteed residency in your home for as long as you wish. Otherwise, your son or daughter might become divorced at a future date and you could be forced to vacate your home as part of some property settlement.

Having reviewed the various possibilities for turning your home into an income producer, you might well come to the conclusion that it still isn't worth it to stay where you are. The prospect of less hassle and less expense and more sunshine or activities might convince you that moving out is the best thing to do. The next two chapters should help you make a move in the right direction.

5
Moving:
decisions, decisions

Once you've made up your mind to move, you'll have to make many important decisions before finally settling on your new home.

Move near or far?

Your first decision probably will involve choosing between staying near your home base or heading for some relatively distant spot. If moving to a better climate is not a major element in your decision-making process, you might want to investigate the possibility of less expensive, easier to manage housing near your current neighborhood. You could save considerable money and still have your comfortable "social network" intact. Doctors' offices, part-time jobs, close friends, and other elements of your emotional and financial make-up would still be there when you needed them.

So, don't throw over the old neighborhood without a thorough inspection of what else is available locally. You might find something that is just right for your retirement plans.

If you're looking for an area with a better climate, lower living costs, more social activities, or whatever, do some solid research. Visit the community or better yet, rent for a while. Subscribe to the town newspaper. Get to know the place and the people before you make a final move. Table 2 at the end of the chapter shows how the average cost of living for middle-income retired people varies in different parts of the country.

Whether you move near or far, you should make sure that your new home has desirable features, particularly those features that are important for your health and safety as you grow older. Use Worksheet 5 at the end of the chapter to evaluate new housing.

Rent or buy?

Another decision you might have to make involves choosing between renting or buying. Something can be said for both. Owning tends to tie you down. If you feel you might be moving again in a few years, renting might be the more economical way to go. Buying and selling homes can be costly if you don't stay put very long.

Owning a home certainly helps those who have to pay a good chunk of their income for taxes. But, at this stage, you may not be in a high-enough tax bracket to need much of a tax shelter. To figure your tax bracket, divide your gross tax (federal and state) by your taxable income. For example, if your combined gross tax is $4,000 and your taxable income is $16,000, your tax bracket would be 25 percent. In general tax shelters become important when you are in the 33 percent bracket or higher. A visit with an accountant or other tax-planning specialist can square you away on this matter.

Even if you do need tax breaks, you can find them elsewhere. You don't have to own a home. You can buy other real estate tax shelters in the form of limited partnerships (more on this in Chapter 11).

Renting a place involves just a small initial investment. You pay the first month's rent plus some sort of security deposit and that's it. No down payment is required, as is usually the case with buying a house or condominium.

When you rent, monthly costs are easier to predict. Maintenance and repairs are usually handled by the landlord. There's no outside upkeep and you can come and go as you please. When you want to travel, you just lock up your apartment and go.

The disadvantages of renting are fairly obvious. You don't own the place and, therefore, you're not building any equity. If you need a tax shelter, you have to get it through some other form of investment. You may be restricted as to how much, if at all, you can modify your unit to suit your tastes. Your activities may also be restricted (no pets, no children). And, of course, there's that old landlord-tenant threat of eviction hanging over your head. You may settle in and find out the building will soon be converted into condominium units. You either pay up as a purchaser or get out. Some of these converted condos are good buys; some are not.

Another problem with renting is finding a decent place at a decent price. In recent years rents have been increasing 10 percent or more yearly, even in rent-controlled areas. Because of the past squeeze on construction, it's a landlord's market in many areas. "Take it or leave it," you are told when an inflated price is quoted. Others are lined up behind you, willing to pay.

You may be able to get a much better place, more suitable to your needs, by purchasing a condominium unit. You get many of the advantages of renting plus the advantages of ownership. You can lock the door and take off when you want to travel. Much of the maintenance and repair cost is budgeted for you in the monthly condo fee. And, these days, you can find units that don't require large down payments (some don't require *any* down payment).

Share ownership or rental costs?
You might want to consider joining forces with other people to buy or rent housing that otherwise would be too expensive for you.

Shared equity
The concept of shared equity is really catching on in some areas. It involves teaming up with an investor for the purchase

of a home (usually a condominium or a house). You become half owner and half tenant. The investor becomes half owner and half landlord. You get a place that usually costs less than renting, and the investor gets a significant tax break, which provides a profit of 16 to 20 percent a year on the investment.

According to Agnes Davis, a nationally known real estate expert who specializes in shared equity investments, here's how a typical deal could go:

"Let's say the condominium unit costs $100,000. If you put in $10,000 as a down payment, you get a better rate on the mortgage. Because you're going in with an investor, the down payment only costs you $5,000. The investor, who also acts as cosigner on the loan, usually is well established financially. This means you should have no problem qualifying for a $90,000 loan.

"You share the $900 monthly mortgage payment with the investor, which means you put in $450. Because the investor is half landlord, you also have to pay a monthly rent of, say, $150, making your total monthly outlay $600. But you're paying for half the mortgage, so you will have a nice tax deduction for your share of the interest. And you can deduct half the property taxes. All told, you might come out with a net monthly outlay of only $450 or so. This probably will be a good bit less than you'd pay as a renter. The investor gets good income and a tax break. You get an apartment you otherwise might not have been able to afford. You also get an investment that should keep building in value over the years."

On the other side of the coin, if you already have a home you like and are looking for places to invest your money, you might want to consider becoming a shared equity investor. Consult a tax accountant. A shared equity investment could provide some major tax deductions—a plus for investors who are in high tax brackets.

Most shared equity contracts allow either the investor

or resident to buy the other out according to a predetermined formula. There should be no problem if the resident wants to move. If the place is sold, the investor collects one-half of any profit that's made.

When you ask a real estate agent or builder about the possibility of shared equity financing, you might get a blank stare. Not everyone in the business knows about it. But be patient and search out someone else in the community who does know (law firm, real estate company, or lender).

If you can't find a shared equity expert nearby, you can get a referral list from Ken Harney, a well-known real estate columnist and author. While you're at it, you might also obtain Harney's book *Profits and Pitfalls: What Every Home Buyer Needs to Know About Equity Sharing.* You get a complete explanation of how equity sharing works, plus the latest referral list and some caveats. For more information on Harney's referral list and the book, write: Harney Corporation, Box 4036, Chevy Chase, MD 20815.

If you do decide to try equity sharing with an investor, make sure you have a lawyer look over the contract. The lawyer should have had experience with shared equity contracts. In the past, some hopeful buyers have been taken in by unscrupulous investors who demanded half payment from residents but gave them less than half ownership. This type of situation, which might occur when buildings are being converted from rental to condominium units, should never happen if you have an experienced lawyer's assistance. Contracts should also include protection against the possibility that an investor might default on payments.

There are other ways to share the cost of ownership (or the cost of renting), but they're not as neat and tidy.

Rent a group house
If you want to rent, you might consider going in with a group to rent an entire house instead of a single apartment unit for yourself.

Because others are involved, this takes some doing. But, presuming you are able to come up with two or three kindred souls (or another couple), you can shop around for a potential group-living house in a nice neighborhood. The house might be unaffordable and too big for one person or a couple. With four people going in together, it might be just right. Rent, utilities, even major food purchases can be split four ways. Household chores can be divided or a housekeeper can do the work, with the cost being divided up among the residents. The major advantages to group living are lower monthly expenses and the security and companionship that come from a small "community."

The major disadvantage is obvious. You lose some of your privacy and independence. You may have been a beneficient dictator in your previous family home. You ran the kitchen and all that went with it. Now, you have to share this leadership with others. For some people, this can become intolerable. You may want the furniture one way, and someone else may want it the other way. You've got to have a compatible group or things can go sour.

Some zoning laws may prohibit or restrict the use of group living arrangements. Always check on this before you try to form a group.

To help you grapple with the potential for group living, there's a recent book on the subject called *The Group House Handbook* (Acropolis), by Nancy Brandwein, Jill McNeice, and Peter Spiers (three people who formed their own home-rental community). There's a chapter called "Group Housing for Seniors."

You're usually better off with group living arrangements if you can get a community organization such as your church, synagogue, club, association, or local service agency to help screen applicants and provide administrative support. And better yet, the organization might own the property so that all residents are renters. Although considerable care must be taken in forming a group, there are lots of successful

$$$

48 **What to do with what you've got**

examples that prove it can work and work well. The Shared
Housing Resource Center, 6344 Green Street, Philadelphia,
PA 19144, has a manual to help groups get together and
get underway.

Buy a group house

It's also possible for a compatible group to purchase a home.
This requires careful legal supervision (each group member
should have his or her own lawyer). If four people band
together to buy a home, the down payment and monthly
payments are split four ways. Here's how Tish Sommers,
president of the Older Women's League, describes her com-
munity purchase arrangement with three other women:

"It wasn't easy. We had to learn to live together.
Women tend to clash if they ran their own homes before.
. . . Privacy is important. Each of us had our own room
or room-and-a-half. We had a common dining and living
room and kitchen space. You have to work out the manage-
ment, cleanliness, chores. . . . It took about six months before
we ironed out all our differences. After we got organized,
it worked very well. . . . We supported each other and it
made living costs much less expensive."

Contracts for shared ownership

There are three basic ways to write up contracts for shared
ownership of a residential property:

Joint tenancy Each owner shares equally in the building.
In the event of a death, that person's share is automatically
passed to the other owner or owners without going through
probate proceedings.

Tenancy in common Each owner has the right to specify
in a will who each wishes his or her share to go to. Each
owner also has the right to sell, mortgage, or give away the
share owned.

Partnership The building is owned by the partnership, not by the individual partners. How partners will share in ownership and management is spelled out in the contract. If one partner dies, the heirs acquire the interest and any incumbent obligations. This type of ownership is recommended when one partner is an investor who will not live on the property, and when the age difference between partners is great.

There are two important points to consider before you enter into shared ownership: (1) In most states, you are liable for the total mortgage debt if you sign the mortgage agreement—no matter how the title is held. (2) A partnership contract can offer some legal protection in cases of bankruptcy, debts, or divorce.

Compare various housing modes

So far, our investigation of possible places to live has centered primarily on rental apartments, rental houses, condominium units, and various shared equity or shared living schemes. Here's a quick primer on how these various housing modes might stack up:

Condominiums

Condo units are available in many parts of the country and are relatively easy to buy. You can obtain regular mortgage financing and get a deed of ownership for your unit; you share ownership of common areas. There are all sorts of disclosure documents condominium developers must provide—by law. Gather this information and study it. When you buy a condo from a second owner, the disclosure documents may or may not be provided—this varies from state to state. If you're serious about buying a unit, have your lawyer go over the condominium contract and bylaws. Remember, you're not just buying a home, you're buying into an active business that you and the other owners have to manage as a group.

Cooperatives

Co-ops are similar to condominiums in the sense that you have the right to live in one specific unit. But you don't actually own the unit, as you do with a condominium. Instead, you own a share in the building and grounds, sort of like a share of stock. One mortgage covers everything. This share can be bought and sold, but lenders are often leery about providing long-term financing for this share, making it more difficult to sell when you want to move out. Legislation has been proposed which would give co-op owners a type of deed similar to those provided condo owners. With this type of arrangement, lenders would be more willing to make long-term financing for co-op shares.

Mobile homes

You can still find plenty of fancy mobile home "community" parks in California, Florida, and elsewhere. You own your unit, which is now called a "manufactured home," but you usually don't own the land it sits on. You rent that. People who like the community spirit of a mobile home park swear by it. Others find there's a lack of privacy. Check with several residents, and their past experiences, before you take the plunge. Where laws permit, some manufactured home communities sell you the land and the home in a package, much like a traditionally built house. You get a permanent foundation and may be able to obtain long-term VA or FHA mortgage financing for about one-third less than that for a similar home built in the conventional manner. For more information, write: Manufactured Housing Institute, 1745 Jefferson Davis Highway, Arlington, VA 22202.

Life care (continuing care) homes

These units are offered to people who need, or believe they will benefit from, a sheltered living environment with nursing medical facilities available and other "coping" services. For a hefty initial payment (from $30,000 on up) plus a monthly fee ($400 and up), you get a living unit with various amenities (cleaning services, maybe a pool, common dining room, activities). It's sort of a hotel for older people with nursing facilities and other standby help. It's not a nursing home. And it's not a free-wheeling retirement community. Something in between.

Life care contracts are intricate, and you might commit a lot of money for something that may not turn out to be what you wanted after all. Some continuing care communities now will refund in full any entrance fee when the life care contract is terminated, but others will not. Always have an attorney look over any form of life care contract. For an informative booklet, *Continuing Care Homes,* write: American Association of Homes for the Aging, 1050 17th Street, N.W., Washington, DC 20036. The booklet has an excellent checklist for your lawyer to use to evaluate prospective life-care contracts.

Ready resources

Inter-City Cost of Living Indicators. Quarterly issued by the American Chamber of Commerce Researchers Association giving detailed cost-of-living statistics on 230 U.S. cities. Provides both index comparisons and actual price figures. Available in libraries.

Finding Your Best Place to Live in America (Red Lion Books) by Thomas F. Bourman, et al., describes and compares 80 different areas across the United States.

Place Rated Almanac (Rand McNally), by Richard Boyer and David Savagean, lists thousands of facts about 277 U.S. metropolitan areas.

Table 2   What about living costs?

Here are sample annual budgets for a middle-income retired couple, according to 1981 statistics from the Department of Labor. They should be updated for inflation, but they do show how living costs can vary.

Area	Total budget	Total consumption
Urban United States	$ 10,226	$ 9,611
Metropolitan areas	10,568	9,932
Nonmetropolitan areas	9,203	8,650
Northeast		
Boston, Mass.	11,925	11,208
Buffalo, N.Y.	10,744	10,098
New York—Northeast N.J.	11,623	10,924
Philadelphia, Pa.—N.J.	10,646	10,006
Pittsburgh, Pa.	10,503	9,871
Nonmetropolitan areas	10,318	9,697
North Central		
Chicago, Ill.—Northwest Ind.	10,070	9,464
Cincinnati, Ohio—Ky.—Ind.	10,038	9,434
Cleveland, Ohio	10,500	9,868
Detroit, Mich.	10,395	9,770
Kansas City, Mo.—Kans.	9,978	9,378
Milwaukee, Wis.	10,673	10,031
Minneapolis—St. Paul, Minn.	10,121	9,512
St. Louis, Mo.—Ill.	10,108	9,500
Nonmetropolitan areas	9,298	8,739
South		
Atlanta, Ga.	9,516	8,944
Baltimore, Md.	10,051	9,446
Dallas, Tex.	9,768	9,180
Houston, Tex.	9,996	9,395
Washington, D.C.—Md.—Va.	11,000	10,338
Nonmetropolitan areas	8,801	8,272
West		
Denver, Colo.	10,028	9,425
Los Angeles—Long Beach, Calif.	10,238	9,622
San Diego, Calif.	9,827	9,236
San Francisco—Oakland, Calif.	10,921	10,264
Seattle—Everett, Wash.	11,343	10,661
Honolulu, Hawaii	12,157	11,426
Nonmetropolitan areas	9,529	8,956
Anchorage, Alaska	12,900	12,124

Worksheet 5   Desirable housing features

Use this checklist to help you evaluate prospective new housing. It's also a useful tool to evaluate your present housing for its suitability for later years.

Houses

Yes No   **Exterior**
☐ ☐ Crack-free foundation
☐ ☐ Smooth walls and paint job
☐ ☐ Roof in good condition
☐ ☐ Gutters/downspouts in good condition
☐ ☐ Adequate drainage of lot
☐ ☐ Adequate parking
☐ ☐ Healthy trees and shrubs
☐ ☐ Storm windows
☐ ☐ Quiet neighborhood

            Floor plan
☐ ☐ Entrance hall, with closet
☐ ☐ Safe stairs
☐ ☐ Large living room
☐ ☐ Well-located bathrooms
☐ ☐ Double-duty room, such as a study-bedroom

            Kitchen/family room
☐ ☐ Adequate counter and shelf space
☐ ☐ Convenient placement of sink, range, refrigerator
☐ ☐ Exhaust fan
☐ ☐ Adequate lighting
☐ ☐ Appliances in good condition
☐ ☐ Adequate work space in laundry area
☐ ☐ Dishwasher garbage disposer

Worksheet 5 Desirable housing features

Houses

Yes No   **Other rooms**
☐ ☐ Adequate, well-lit closets
☐ ☐ Bathroom on each floor, with ventilation
☐ ☐ Adequate wall space for placing furniture
☐ ☐ "Quiet" plumbing and heating systems

Miscellaneous areas
☐ ☐ Linen closet near bedrooms/bath
☐ ☐ Stairs to attic storage
☐ ☐ Wide basement entrance
☐ ☐ No moisture or mildew in closets/basement
☐ ☐ Adequate space for workshop if wanted

Structural mechanical
☐ ☐ Floors in good condition
☐ ☐ Smooth walls and ceilings; no sign of water damage
☐ ☐ Easily opened and locked windows
☐ ☐ Airtight windows and doors; good condition
☐ ☐ 100–200 amp electrical service
☐ ☐ Circuit-breaker panel, six or more circuits
☐ ☐ Adequate water pressure
☐ ☐ 40-gallon water heater
☐ ☐ Well insulated, no drafts
☐ ☐ Girders in good condition
☐ ☐ Adequate heating system
☐ ☐ Sufficient number of electrical outlets

Worksheet 5   Desirable housing features

Apartments

Yes No

☐ ☐ Building well kept, inside and outside
☐ ☐ Well-lit hallways
☐ ☐ Elevator in building, if appropriate
☐ ☐ Quiet neighbors
☐ ☐ Laundry facilities in building
☐ ☐ Adequate parking
☐ ☐ Adequate closet and storage space

Housing for later years

Yes No

☐ ☐ Transportation and shopping facilities nearby
☐ ☐ Rooms on same level, with no walking hazards
☐ ☐ Nonskid floors
☐ ☐ High intensity light
☐ ☐ Night lights in bedroom and bathroom
☐ ☐ Plugs 28–30 inches from floor
☐ ☐ Easy-to-reach storage facilities
☐ ☐ Shower with nonskid floors
☐ ☐ Low bathtub with grab bars and seat ledge
☐ ☐ Cheerful, bright rooms
☐ ☐ Laundry facilities in building
☐ ☐ Recreational facilities in building

6
Selling, buying, moving

The more information you gather, the better armed you will be to handle the hassles and anxiety that go with the whole selling-buying-moving trauma. Without question, you should obtain competent legal and financial advice at every step along the way.

Tax breaks for sellers

After age 55, you might be eligible to receive a handsome tax break when you sell your home. If you make a net profit (capital gain) on the sale, you may exempt up to $125,000 from taxation.

Before you sell your home, it's always wise to have a tax expert look over your current financial situation. You can take the $125,000 exemption only once in your lifetime. If you're not making much of a gain on the current home sale, it might be a poor time to use your exemption. You might be better off saving it for some future date.

Before an older homeowner marries, the one-shot tax exemption situation should be reviewed carefully. If you marry someone who has already taken the big tax exemption, marriage nullifies your right to do likewise. The IRS considers a married couple as one person. The thing to do is to sell your home before you marry. If both partners own homes, both homes can be sold before marriage for a whopping exemption of up to $250,000. The happy pair can buy a new place and bank their tax exemption bonanza.

Remember, you're only taxed on the net profit (capital gain) from your sale. The initial purchase price of the house plus additions or other improvements plus sales costs (fix-up bills, broker's commission, closing) can be added up as your overall cost. This entire "basis" cost can be deducted from the sale price to arrive at your taxable net profit. Here's how it might work:

Let's say you paid $60,000 for your home way back when. It's now being sold for $200,000, giving you a gross profit of $140,000. But let's also say you've spent a total of $15,000 in additions, fixing the place up for sale, and other sales costs. This knocks the taxable net profit down to $125,000. Your exemption wipes that off the slate and you get to keep the entire gross profit tax free.

If your spouse dies, you may get a step up in the tax basis cost. With a jointly owned home in most states, the surviving spouse can use half the current market value as the deceased partner's basis cost. This can greatly elevate the total basis cost, wiping out much, if not all, of the tax that otherwise might have been due.

Example: A couple bought a house years ago for $100,000. They put $40,000 worth of improvements into it. This makes the basis cost $140,000. But one spouse dies and his or her half of the basis cost is calculated at one-half the *current* market value (now $400,000), or $200,000. The surviving partner has a basis cost of $70,000 (half the initial purchase price plus half the additions). Combined, this gives a total basis cost of $270,000, which is deducted from the $400,000 sale price, leaving $130,000 profit. But, the surviving spouse, being over age 55, takes his or her $125,000 exemption, which leaves only $5,000 to be taxed. Because this is a long-term capital gain, and not ordinary income, only 40 percent of the amount ($2,000 in this instance) is subject to tax. And since the top income tax rate now is 50 percent, no matter how large your income, the tax cannot be more than 50 percent, or $1,000. Imagine, paying only $1,000 in taxes on a $400,000 sale. It's awesome what Congress has done for homeowners—especially older homeowners.

Selling your home

When you sell your home, you have to decide early on whether you want to have a professional real estate agent do the job for a commission (usually 6 or 7 percent of the sale price), do it yourself, or do it yourself with limited help from a "discount" or "flat-fee" broker.

Unless you are prepared to put a good amount of time and energy into becoming your own sales agent, it's probably better to let a pro handle the job. You will have plenty of other demands on your time and won't want to deal with advertising, showing, and coping with complicated financing proposals. But if you'd like to do some things yourself and get limited help from a firm, you can get good advice from Peter Miller's book *How to Save Money When You Hire a Real Estate Broker* (Springfield Press, P.O. Box 1762, Silver Spring, MD 20902). Miller also details possible ways to negotiate commissions.

Hire a pro

When you pick a real estate professional, try to get at least two or three recommendations from a lawyer, banker, lender, and others who may know a lot about the local housing business. If you're confused by some of the professional titles, here's a quick rundown:

Real estate agent This person has taken and passed a state board examination involving such things as property laws, financing, and taxes.

Realtor Any licensed agent who joins the National Association of Realtors can call himself or herself a Realtor (a trademark name). The organization has a code of ethics members are supposed to follow.

Real estate broker This person has taken a more comprehensive state board examination and passed it. Brokers often run real estate offices with licensed agents doing most of the sales work. Brokers are responsible for approving and signing sales contracts and listing forms.

Before you make your final selection, have each prospective sales agent come by your home to make a thorough inspection and suggest a competitive sale price. Each sales agent should make a proposal describing how he or she plans to sell your home. It should include an advertising budget and special sales methods (some provide prospective buyers with fact sheets or brochures on your home). How many homes does the agent's firm have for sale in your area? How many have been sold? You should know which agents and their firms have the most sales and most experience in your neighborhood.

Out of all this, you should be able to settle on one firm, and one representative of that firm, who you feel can do a good job.

Sign a listing contract

In signing a contract, you want to give the firm enough time to do a proper selling job, but not so much time as to tie you up in case you want to make a change to another company later on. Sixty days is a fair turn at bat. If you like the broker or agent, and your home is still unsold, you can renew for another sixty days.

Ask about the exclusivity clause. Does the firm want exclusive listing? Or will the home be put on multiple listing to be shared with other firms in the area? You might want to compromise and offer a brief period of exclusive listing after which you would be plugged into multiple listing. Most real estate experts say multiple listing is the better way to go. More firms will be out there trying to sell your home. It's not a bad idea to have your contract inspected by an attorney before you sign.

With both exclusive listing and multiple listing contracts, the listing firm has the right to obtain a commission on the sale of your home even if you sell it yourself during the contract period. You might want to negotiate an open listing contract, in which you hire brokers on a nonexclusive basis, or an exclusive agency contract, in which you agree to have only one firm represent you. With both types you can also sell your home yourself without paying a commission.

Spruce up your home
A good agent will tell you how to spruce up your home to make it more attractive to potential buyers. A coat of paint here, a new fixture there, carpet cleaning, flowers strategically placed should do it. Remember, the amount spent on the spruce-up job can be added to your overall basis cost to reduce the tax you might have to pay. You shouldn't invest a lot of money in improvements, though, as you won't get your money back in the sales price.

The offer to buy
Once a buyer makes a firm offer on your home in a written offer-to-buy contract, you should give it serious consideration even though it's below your asking price. If the buyer has good financial backing (can get a loan), you might want to reduce your price to make a quick sale. Remember, an unsold home costs money. All your expenses continue.

"Don't be greedy," real estate expert Agnes Davis says, explaining that "some homeowners emotionally overvalue their homes and sit on them far too long." Eventually, she says, "they end up selling for a lower price anyway, losing a lot of money in the process."

Financing arrangements

Any offer-to-buy contract should be reviewed by your attorney. This is especially true if "creative financing" methods are proposed. This type of financing requires you, the seller, to become a lender. Lending on today's terms can be a complicated business. A lawyer should guide you all the way through the final sale and closing procedures. Ideally the lawyer will be well versed in real estate financing. When you deal with a lawyer and a real estate firm, here's some of the financing jargon you might hear:

Seller take back If you still have a considerable amount to pay on your mortgage, you take back a second mortgage or deed of trust to help the buyer assume your existing loan. There's usually a large gap between your selling price and the amount left to pay on the mortgage. The buyer puts some money down and gets you to loan the rest.

Balloon payment The buyer can pay back the amount you lend with installments over several years and one large "balloon" payment at the end.

Blended mortgage Your lender agrees to let the buyer assume your mortgage at a higher rate than you're paying but at a lower rate than is generally being charged in the market. Or the lender issues a new mortgage at the blended rate. The buyer pays a healthy amount down and you finance the remainder over the next couple of years.

Regular cash contract (the way it used to be) An ideal situation. The buyer has been able to get a full mortgage and can pay you off completely. You get all your money out and do not have to become a reluctant lender.

There are several other twists and turns in the financing field, but these examples should give you some sort of basis for asking questions. Your real estate agent and lawyer should be able to spell out any type of fancy financing arrangements to your satisfaction.

Buying a home
When you've sold your home and become a buyer for your next home, you may want to put as little money down as possible or you may want to put a large amount down. It depends on your tax status, the amount of money you have, and the cost of your loan.

If you can get a seller to help with the financing, you might get a lower interest rate on the loan. If you can get your own financing, however, you may be better off in the long run. In most cases you should try to get a traditional fixed-rate 25- or 30-year mortgage, which is becoming available again. With an adjustable rate mortgage (ARM), you may pay the same money each month, but the amount of interest and principal payments may be juggled back and forth, depending on the current interest rate situation. Or your monthly payments may fluctuate. ARMs are usually not recommended for retirees on fixed incomes. An attorney and real estate agent should be able to steer you clear of any type of dangerous or otherwise unattractive financing.

Once the deal has been signed, your next steps are to arrange to move in and to have the structure and your belongings insured.

Moving
You can now get a fixed price on an interstate move. Prior to government deregulation of the industry, moving companies were not allowed to give fixed prices on interstate transfers of goods. They had to adhere to rigid "tariffs." Deregulation permits much more price competition for your business. This is why you should interview at least two or three moving

companies before you select the one you want for the job. On local moves, not governed by interstate regulations, companies have always been able to make competitive bids and quote fixed prices.

On interstate moves you can now get replacement-value insurance from the mover. With a $250 deductible (they pay everything over that amount), you can keep the cost down. The old method of insuring a move is still available. But it's not such a good buy because you're paid off with a depreciated value. You're better off with replacement value and a deductible.

On an interstate move, the companies must provide government-required disclosure booklets. Read them carefully. On local moves, your county or city consumer protection agency (if there is one) should have a guide that spells out local rules and may even have a list of companies about which they're received customer complaints. If your mover has an iffy record, you'll be told. The same kind of service may be available from your local Better Business Bureau.

Homeowners and renters insurance

The big thing to remember is that in most states your insurance must be sufficient to cover at least 80 percent of the replacement value of your home (this should include the structure(s), not the land and foundation). If you fall below the 80 percent level, the insurance company may pay part of your loss, but not all.

Consider getting an inflation-escalator clause to make sure your property meets the 80 percent cutoff limit. You can cut premium costs by absorbing larger deductibles.

Homeowners insurance usually covers the furniture and other belongings at a figure based on 50 percent of the home's insured value.

If you are renting a home, you should get renters or

tenants insurance, which covers the value of your belongings—not the structure (which is covered by the building owner).

If you move out of a home you own and rent it to someone else, your homeowners policy is no longer valid. You must get a "fire-broad-form" policy which covers the structure only. The contents are supposedly covered by the tenant. If you take out a new homeowners policy for your new home, you can get an endorsement that covers you for liability on your old home-rental property.

Inventory of belongings
You should record all your furniture and other property room by room in an updated inventory. Some owners are using small video cameras or still cameras for this job (along with the traditional explanatory notes, receipts, and appraisals).

Home sweet home?
To help you sort out all your stay-put, rent, sell, buy options, use Worksheet 6 at the end of this chapter to compare costs.

Ready resources

Housing as We Grow Older. A largish booklet on the whole subject of staying put, moving out, buying, renting, and special housing. For information on how to obtain a copy, write: Cornell Distribution Center, 7 Research Park, Ithaca, NY 14850.

Home Buyer's Checklist. A small book written by real estate attorney Benny L. Kass. The book provides easy-to-read tips on buying a home from a lawyer's viewpoint. Mr. Kass is coauthor of another useful book, **Condo Owners Guide.** For information on obtaining the books, write: National Home Buyers and Home Owners Association, Washington, DC 20036.

Buyer's Guide to Insurance. This booklet includes a section on homeowners or renters insurance with a checklist of "Buying Hints." For more information, write: National Insurance Consumer Organization, 344 Commerce Avenue, Alexandria, VA 22314.

Policy Wise: The Practical Guide to Insurance Decisions for Older Consumers. An AARP Book by consumer protection attorney Nancy H. Chasen, **Policy Wise** is an excellent resource guide for making life, health, residential, and automobile insurance choices. See Chapter 13 for information on how to order.

Worksheet 6   Stay put or move?

Possible Expenses	Possible Bonuses

Stay put

Possible Expenses	Possible Bonuses
$ ___Mortgage, rent	$ ___Estimated equity
___Property taxes	___Tax deduction for
___Property insurance	mortgage interest
___Maintenance	___Estimated annual
___Utilities	appreciation
___Major repairs	___State or local tax
___Condo, co-op,	breaks for seniors
mobile home fees	___Renting rooms for
	income

Sell

Possible Expenses	Possible Bonuses
$ ___Sprucing-up costs	$ ___Net profit after
___Broker's fee	deducting expenses
___Legal fees,	and tax benefits
closing costs	
___Any capital	
gains taxes	
___Financing costs	

Rent it out

Possible Expenses	Possible Bonuses
$ ___Mortgage payments	$ ___Rental income
___Property taxes	___Tax benefits
___Maintenance	(depreciation)
___Liability, fire	___Tax deductions
insurance	for mortgage
___Taxes on net	interest
rental income	___Estimated
___Possible loss of	equity
capital gains	___Estimated annual
tax breaks	appreciation

Worksheet 6   Stay put or move?

Possible Expenses	Possible Bonuses

Move

$ ___Mover's fees	$ ___Garage sale of
___Travel costs	unwanted belongings

Buy

$ ___Cash in full	$ ___Equity
___Down payment	___Estimated
___Mortgage	appreciation
payments	___Tax deductions
___Property taxes	for mortgage interest
___Homeowners	___Defer capital
insurance	gains tax
___Maintenance	___State or local tax
___Utilities	breaks for senior
___Condo, co-op	homeowners
fees	

Rent

$ ___Deposit	$ ___Net profit on
___Rent payments	sale of old home
___Utilities	___State or local tax
___No federal	breaks for senior
tax deductions	renters
___Renters insurance	___No maintenance
___Loss of capital	costs or headaches
gains tax defferal	___No property tax
___No equity	
appreciation	

7
Savings revolution

As we've seen, a home can turn out to be a major source of investment funds. Once you've appraised your home situation to see if money can be made on your equity, your next step is to determine what you can do with your savings accounts, stocks, bonds, and the like. Your goal is to always do better with what you've got. *Don't* lose money on risky investments. *Do* make as much as you can while giving yourself as much flexibility and as little risk exposure as possible. By this we mean don't tie up too much, if any, money in hard-to-sell or hard-to-cash-in investments. For the most part, you want to stay as liquid as possible (have quick and easy access to your money).

Fortunately, you're now witnessing a major revolution in the banking-savings industry. The government is plucking away regulations that limit how much an institution may pay its depositors. (Credit unions are, for the most part, completely deregulated.) This has created a considerable amount of intramural competition among the various institutions, and outside competition with the unregulated money market mutual fund industry.

Savings options
Once upon a time, savings options were limited. Banks and savings and loans offered passbook accounts that paid relatively low interest (5 percent plus) but generally allowed withdrawals without any penalty. To get higher interest, you had

to agree to leave your money in a time deposit account for periods of up to four years or so. If you withdrew your money before the stipulated time, you were assessed a penalty on the interest paid.

Then along came money market mutual funds. Not regulated as were banks, these funds were allowed to offer what, in effect, were high-flying passbook accounts with no limits on withdrawals. You could earn high interest and take your money out any time—without penalty. Investors flocked to money market funds.

To lure depositors back to financial institutions, the government allowed institutions to issue certificates of deposit (CDs) with competitive interest rates and the added advantage of government insurance. CDs became popular but still had the drawbacks of restricted access and penalties for early withdrawal—just like the older time deposit accounts.

Congress stepped in to even up the competition between financial institutions and money market funds. Now, you can get money market-type savings accounts at banks and savings and loans that let you withdraw your money without penalty and still earn high interest rates.

Money market accounts vs. funds

With the financial institution money market accounts, your deposit is insured by a federal agency up to $100,000. Private money market mutual funds are not insured by the government. (Some funds offer private insurance.) But there's a catch with the bank money market accounts. You must ante up a minimum of $2,500 to open up the account. Then you must maintain that minimum balance of $2,500 or lose your high interest rate (you get the old, low passbook rate). Money market funds have no minimum balance requirement—an important selling point. And, with some of the money market funds, such as the one offered by AARP, your initial deposit can be as little as $500.

If maintaining a balance of $2,500 in a financial institution account bothers you, try a money market fund. To get a list of money market fund names, addresses, and investment information, write: Investment Company Institute, 1775 K Street, N.W., Washington, DC 20006. Most funds have toll-free 800 numbers.

What about the insured deposit angle? Sophisticated investors don't pay a lot of attention to that. They realize that you can get your money out so fast (just a phone call) there's virtually no risk. According to the Investment Company Institute, the trade association for money market funds, "not one penny has ever been lost in a money market fund." The funds invest in short-term obligations (30 to 90 days) that are issued by the Treasury, by banks, and by corporations. They are virtually risk free.

One caveat: Be a little wary of any fund that offers a rate considerably above the others. It may be investing heavily in somewhat risky commercial paper (short-term corporate debt obligations) or in longer term obligations that could suffer if interest rates go up substantially. When you ask a money market fund for information, it must send you a prospectus (by law) which shows all the fund's short-term investments. Look it over. But, remember, to date nobody has lost a penny in a money market fund.

The absolute safest funds, if that's what you're looking for, are those that invest most, if not all, of their cash in short-term Treasury obligations. These funds may pay slightly less interest than those with primarily commercial portfolios, but you get maximum safety.

Some enterprising money market funds are offering new "combination" accounts. The fund invests your deposits above $2,500 in a government-insured money market account (through the fund's affiliation with a bank or savings and loan). The moment your deposit sinks below $2,500, your money is automatically switched to the companion money market fund where it earns high interest. Your rate never drops down to the otherwise required 5 percent plus passbook rate. Of course, when your cash is in the money market fund, it's not federally insured. But, so what? The risk of loss is infinitessimal.

Certificates of deposit
Besides the newer money market accounts, financial institutions still offer passbook accounts and the longer term certificates of deposits mentioned earlier. The CDs have fixed rates that can be locked up for one month on out to three and one-half years or more. CDs may be paying a higher rate than money market accounts. Depends on market conditions.

 If you don't need your money right away, you can let it ride in a certificate for thirty days, three months, six months, a year, or longer. The minimum initial deposit is $2,500. The longer the term the higher the interest rate. If interest rates go down, you're ahead of the game. If they go up, you're stuck with a lower rate for a while. If you do invest in CDs, plan ahead. You'll have to forfeit some interest as penalty if you need to cash the CD in before maturity.

Checking options
The higher interest wave has also engulfed the checking account business. At first, financial institutions offered NOW (Negotiable Order of Withdrawal) accounts that allowed you to get interest on your checking balance. Initially, this rate was the traditional passbook rate of 5 percent plus. Later on, institutions were allowed to pay any interest they wanted on NOW accounts if the depositor's balance was maintained above a $2,500 cutoff. But, because these Super NOW accounts were more expensive to operate, they paid less interest than money market accounts or funds.

 This is when sophisticated depositors started to use

all sorts of switching ploys to get top interest and check-writing privileges to boot. Most money market funds will let you write checks for $250 or $500 at a time. You maintain a small balance (a few hundred dollars) in a free or low-cost checking account somewhere and periodically transfer cash from your money market fund to bolster your checking balance. The same trick can be used with an insured money market savings account. You periodically switch high-interest money as needed into your checking account. You are limited to six telephone transfers a month. That's plenty for most checking accounts.

Interest-rate shopping
With a plethora of funds and accounts being offered, what's a depositor to do? One thing you've got to watch out for is the frantic game of interest-rate chasing. You read about one bank offering X percent, so you send your money there. Later, you read about a savings and loan that's offering X plus Y percent, so you switch over there. In the long run, you really don't earn much extra interest and you end up with messy records involving accounts spread all over town. A real bookkeeping chore.

By all means check around town for the best, consistent (underline that word) interest rate and put your money there. If the institution where you've done business for years offers an account with a rate that's close enough to the others, might as well stay put. You are a respected, long-time customer and have some clout that goes with the image. They know you, they like you, they take care of you with personal service.

Credit unions
If you're not pleased with your current institution, you may want to check out the possibility of joining a credit union. These nonprofit savings and lending organizations provide

services only to members, who have some kind of common bond such as employment or community. Deposits in 95 percent of credit unions are insured up to $100,000. Some credit unions offer special services such as financial planning and discount rates on hotels and car rentals. Since credit unions have been deregulated, they're allowed to pay interest rates on accounts as high as they wish to go. But this doesn't mean they always offer the best rates or services. You should comparison shop. For information about credit unions or joining one, write: National Association for Retired Credit Union People, P.O. Box 391, Madison, WI 53701.

Electronic fund transfers
In connection with your savings and/or checking accounts at a financial institution, you may be offered the option of using new services revolving around what is called electronic fund transfers (EFT).

If you opt for EFT services, you'll be given a confidential PIN (personal identification number) and a plastic EFT card. You can pay your bills by phone, punching code numbers into a computer (you need a pushbutton phone). You can make other transactions by phone (from savings to checking and vice versa) or use conveniently located automatic teller machines (ATMs).

In the not-too-distant future, people who use EFT services will be able to activate their various accounts from automatic teller machines all around the country—and eventually, from abroad. If you live in Chicago and you need cash late Sunday night in San Francisco, for example, you'll be able to go to a member bank's ATM, punch in your code, and withdraw the cash you need. Besides the bank networks, banking-type transactions will be offered by the likes of supermarket chains, department stores, and others.

If you decide to use EFT services, be extra careful with your PIN (personal identification number) and EFT card. Anyone who knows your PIN and obtains your EFT card can withdraw money from your account. Memorize your number. Never leave it written down in your wallet or purse. Keep all your ATM transaction receipts and keep a close eye on your monthly statements. Report any discrepancies or any lost or stolen EFT card immediately. Otherwise, you might be liable for a good portion of any money that's withdrawn by unauthorized persons.

Utility company investments

You might want to consider another type of investment that is relatively safe and accessible and pays a higher rate than money market accounts or funds. These flexible, high-interest investments are issued by public utilities in the form of common stock. If you choose carefully, you can buy a utility stock that pays two percentage points or more above the money market rates.

According to Alexandra Armstrong, a certified financial planner with her own money management company, "some investors are putting money into carefully selected utilities to get the highest rate with a certain amount of safety and flexibility."

The utility (usually an electric power company) should be in a growing, fairly recession-proof area and should not be too involved with nuclear power, Armstrong says. If you ask for a special "dividend reinvestment plan" for utility stocks, the tax on your dividends is deferred until you cash in the stock. The amount you can defer in any given year is limited to $750 per person ($1,500 for married couples filing jointly). The utilities' special investment plans can provide yet another tax advantage. If you meet the holding period requirements, you can convert your dividend income to capital gains, which are taxed at a much more favorable rate. To buy utility stocks and to find out about the pros and cons of a specific stock, contact a broker.

8
Stocks and bonds

The utility company stocks discussed in the last chapter are more like savings accounts or money market funds than most other stocks. The better buys with less risk are issued by solid, well-established utility companies. And the price of their stocks doesn't vary all that much. In general, you can get your money out any time you want and probably won't suffer much of a loss, if any. You might even pick up a profit. Meanwhile, you're earning a high rate of return.

Most of the other stocks traded on the New York Stock Exchange, American Exchange, and regional exchanges or those traded "over the counter" (among a network of securities dealers) are another matter. They usually are more susceptible to market swings. You can make money with stock dividends (although not all that much), but you have to pay the full tax load on your earnings.

Growth stocks

"I know most retired customers seem to be interested in securities that provide steady income," says financial planner Alexandra Armstrong, "but they should also consider looking into stocks that have longer term growth potential." She explains her position this way:

"Many retired people are living longer and have many years ahead of them. With longer term growth stocks, they can make money from capital gains (the profit you make when you sell your stock for more than you paid for it). If you've held the stock for more than a year, income tax is calculated on only 40 percent of the profit."

The trick is to find a stock or group of stocks that will increase in value as you grow older. From time to time, you can sell off some shares and use the proceeds as income. It's like pruning a tree that keeps on growing.

In general, if you don't know much about a certain stock, you shouldn't put your money into it. You can't rely on some stockbroker to do all your investing for you. A broker can supply good information such as the size of the company you're investing in, share of the market, dividend background, market outlook, and the like. But you should make the final selection yourself. You need to research individual stocks on your own before you buy. (Table 3 at the end of this chapter shows how to decipher stock quotations in newspapers.)

Investment clubs

One way to gather information about the stock market anu individual securities is to join an investment club. Many retired people are finding that investment clubs combine social pleasure with making a profit. You pay $25 annual dues and your minimum monthly involvement in the club's stock and bond portfolio is $10–$25. It's an inexpensive way to learn plenty about the stock market and have a nice social time while you're at it. Club members usually meet once a month at someone's house for coffee and cake. Each member is responsible for researching a specific security.

Once you've learned quite a bit about a specific stock, or several stocks, you may want to invest more than the monthly minimum. You can also invest outside the club through a broker with your own side bets. Investment club members have done consistently better than the stock market growth average. For more information on how to join or start an investment club, write: National Association of Investment Clubs, P.O. Box 220, Royal Oak, MI 48068. As a member, you'll also get the association's monthly investment magazine.

Mutual funds

Another good way to get into the stock market with some control over the risk factors is to put your money into a good, broad-based, growth-oriented mutual fund. In case you may not already know what a mutual fund is and how it operates, here's a brief rundown.

A mutual fund investment company managed by professionals buys up a large portfolio of stocks and, in some instances, bonds and money market instruments (big bank certificates of deposit, U.S. Treasury offerings, and other short-term, high-interest investments). The idea is to have a highly diversified, flexible portfolio aimed at making a tidy profit over the years. When you buy in as a shareholder, you get your own micro-slices of the total portfolio pie.

Unless you were the next best thing to a millionaire, you would never have enough money to get this kind of diversification. You'd have to be content with a few stocks and this could be dangerous. If one or more of your stocks were to go bad, it would put a big dent in your little portfolio. If one or two stocks go bad in the mutual fund portfolio, there's far less damage, and any loss is more than offset by better performance elsewhere in the portfolio.

Of course, a successful scenario for a mutual fund depends heavily on how well the portfolio is managed. When there's a recession and subsequent downturn in the market, how well do the fund managers get out of sliding stocks and into rising interest rate investments such as money market funds and Treasury offerings? And how well do the fund managers catch a market upturn and get in at a good price with solid stocks?

Some do better than others. You can get help on grading past performance of mutual funds through such publications as the *Handbook for No-Load Investors* and *Forbes* magazine's annual mutual fund issue (September). Some libraries may have one or both of these publications. For more information on the handbook, write: No-Load Fund Investor, P.O. Box 283, Hastings-On-Hudson, NY 10706. When you order the handbook, you also get the *No-Load Investor Newsletter*— the best in the business.

Load or no-load?

Around now you may be wondering what "no-load" means. It's a tag that goes with certain mutual funds that don't charge a sales commission because shares are purchased directly from the company. You order by direct mail and no money has to go to a sales representative such as a stockbroker, insurance salesperson, or financial planner.

Around half of the mutual funds (excluding money market funds, which are always no-load) are now no-load— no commission. The other half are called "load" funds because their shares are sold by sales representatives who nick off 7 to 8 percent commission on each sale.

Why would anyone want to go out of their way to pay a commission when other funds are commission-free? Inertia, perhaps. Someone sells them a fund. They don't go out and buy it. "A good no-load fund," says Sheldon Jacobs, publisher of the *Handbook for No-Load Investors*, "is every bit as good as a load fund—so why pay more?"

You can get a free list of some 700 mutual funds— load and no-load—from the Investment Company Institute, 1775 K Street, N.W., Washington, DC 20006 (the same people who provide the free list of money market mutual funds).

Table 4 at the end of this chapter explains how to decipher mutual fund quotations in newspapers.

Family of funds

Some mutual fund companies offer what they call a "family of funds." This means they have a group of different types of funds under their management. They have, for example, growth stock funds, bond funds, tax-free bond funds, money market funds, energy-related funds, high-technology stock funds—you name it. You can invest in one of the funds and slide part or all of your money over into another one any time you choose. You just pick up the phone and dial a toll-free 800 number and there's usually no charge for the transfer. Some investors have become quite sharp at switching money around in a family of funds. Here's an example:

Let's say you invest in a growth stock fund. The value of your share in an upbeat stock market keeps on growing. But the economy weakens and interest rates start climbing. Generally, when interest rates go up investors tend to shun the stock market and run for cover into some sort of money market investment (money market fund or Treasury bill). As the stock market goes down, they ride the money market investments up. When interest rates start coming down again, they slowly ease back into stocks.

Of course, this somewhat sophisticated game is not for everyone. You have to know how the money markets and securities markets work and you have to keep an eye on interest rate trends—up and down. *The Wall Street Journal* and your newspaper's financial pages can be of help with this.

You can see how much more flexibility you can get with the family of funds concept. At certain times, you may want most of your money in an income-producing fund. You slide into that. Other times, you may want your money in a tax-free bond fund. You slide some money into that. Not all of the family of fund companies have all types of investments. You have to pick and choose. And, of course, some organizations have a better record than others (see the *Forbes* and *No-Load Handbook* ratings).

For your convenience, here's a listing of no-load family of funds organizations provided by the No-load Fund Investor organization. To get the toll-free numbers, dial 800–555–1212 (in some areas it's 1–800–555–1212) and ask for the toll-free-number information operator. If you live near the fund's headquarters, you may have to call direct.

No-load family of funds organizations
Alliance Capital Management—New York
American Investors—Greenwich, Conn.
Babson—Kansas City
Boston Company—Boston
Sull & Bear—New York
Calvert Group—Washington, D.C.
Dreyfus—New York
Fidelity—Boston
Founders Mutual—Denver
United Services Gold Shares—San Antonio
Lehman Management—New York
T. Rowe Price—Baltimore
Pro Services—Flowertown, Pa.
Safeco Asset Management—Seattle
Scudder, Stevens, Clark—Boston
Stein, Rowe, Farnham—Chicago
Stratton—Blue Bell, Pa.
Twentieth Century—Kansas City
Unified—Indianapolis
U.S.A.A. Investment—San Antonio
Value Line—New York
Vanguard—Valley Forge, Pa.
Wood, Struthers, Winthrop—New York

Timing your investment
When you decide to invest in a particular mutual fund that suits your needs for continuing growth you should then consider how best to time your investments. At any given time during a three- or four-year period, the stock market is going to be up—or down. And a growth fund's performance will reflect these ups and downs.

If you plunk a sizable chunk of your cash into a growth fund when it's at or near the top of a stock market cycle, you've usually got no place to go but down for a while. This makes it difficult to come up with a worthwhile profit record. You might even be a loser for a spell.

If you get in at the ground floor, on or near the bottom of a market cycle, you've got it made. But who knows when the bottom of a cycle has hit? Even the experts can never agree when this phenomenon takes place.

Dollar averaging The way around this dilemma is to "dollar average" your investments. You keep a steady flow going into a mutual fund (or individual stocks, if you're taking the independent investment route). This way, you average out your losses and gains. Here's how it might work:

You've decided to put $500 into a specific mutual fund every quarter. The first quarter the market goes up and your $500 investment is now worth $550. But, you have to buy another round, and this time you get fewer shares for your $500. Four months later, however, you send in your $500 and notice that you get more shares than the previous time because the stock market has gone down and you can get more for the same amount of money.

When the market goes up, you feel good because you've made a paper profit. When the market goes down, you feel good because you get your next shares at a discount. Over the years, this form of investing has proven itself to be almost infallible for well-diversified portfolios.

As a retirement income vehicle a mutual fund is much more flexible than an annuity or individual stocks because you can determine just how much income you want mailed to you regularly. Or you can have the income reinvested. You can take all your money out, if need be. And you can switch from one type of mutual fund investment to another.

Bonds

Bonds, or long-term debt obligations, are issued by the U.S. government (*government bonds*), by state and local governments and other political subdivisions (*municipal bonds*), and by companies (*corporate bonds*). U.S. Treasury bonds are considered "safe" investments because they're backed by the "full faith and credit" of the federal government. These are discussed with other government securities in Chapter 9. Other kinds of bonds carry the risk of credit failure—the bond issuer may not be able to pay back the bondholder. Bonds are rated according to risk by two bond rating services: Moody's and Standard & Poor's. Their publications are available at public libraries or brokers. Ratings go from triple A (highest) to C or D (lowest). Experts usually advise buying only triple A bonds or certainly nothing lower than triple B.

     Bonds may be *secured bonds,* backed by specific assets, or *unsecured bonds* (debentures), which are backed only by the reputation and financial position of the issuer. Bonds issued at the same time may all mature at the same time (*term bonds*) or at different dates (*serial bonds*).

How the bond market operates

Any time after a bond is issued, the same issue can be bought or sold in the secondary marketplace—on stock exchanges or over the counter. The price that people are willing to pay for this bond today may be very different from the face value you paid. A bond may sell at a price below face value (a *discount bond*) or above face value (a *premium bond*). Market prices fluctuate depending on current interest rates on newly issued bonds, maturity of a bond, general economic conditions, and specific financial news about a particular bond issuer, affecting the risk or desirability of holding a bond.

     If you buy a bond at face value and hold it to maturity, you are locked in to the same interest rate for the long term (for up to forty years for some bonds). If you buy an original-issue discount bond, you buy at a price at less than face value and redeem it at face value. Your earnings with either type are not affected by changes in the market *unless* you want to sell your bond before maturity, and then the price you receive will be the current market price for your particular bond. But if other issues come along offering higher interest rates or lower original-issue discount prices, you are in effect losing investment potential—you are not receiving the highest return possible on your money. This is the main risk of investing in bonds—long-term fixed returns that may not keep pace with inflation.

Call provisions Bond issuers protect themselves from having to pay high interest rates on older bond issues after they have issued newer bonds with lower interest rates by adding provisions to certain bonds. These provisions give the issuer the right to buy back the bonds at face value plus a premium when interest rates drop. These bonds are called *callable bonds*. To protect your investment you should always check call provisions before you buy bonds.

Municipal bonds and bond funds

Municipal bonds are issued by state and local governments. They are exempt from federal income tax and, if you buy a bond issued in your state, the income may also be exempt from state and local taxes. State laws determine the taxability of these bonds.

You can buy individual municipal bonds through a broker, but this may be a little risky because you get no diversification protection. Perhaps the easiest and safest way to get this kind of tax-free income is to buy into a bond mutual fund or a unit investment trust (a packet of bonds purchased as a group by the fund and held that way until maturity). Bond funds have fluctuating interest rates which reflect the market. Unit trusts offer a fixed rate of return, which can be risky if interest rates go up. Some bond funds are no-load. Others are sold through brokers. If you want a fund with bonds only from your own state, ask a broker what might be available. Table 5 at the end of the chapter

shows the taxable yields that you'd have to earn in your
tax bracket to equal tax-free income.

Corporate bonds

Bonds issued by corporations sometimes pay higher interest
rates than municipal bonds, but they're subject to full federal,
state, and local income taxes. These bonds usually are issued
in denominations of $1,000, but they normally trade on the
stock exchanges or over the counter in minimum amounts
of $5,000 or $10,000. A corporate bond is a company's most
senior security and takes precedence over preferred and common stock.

Corporate bonds are purchased mainly by large investors such as insurance companies and banks, but some people
seeking a conservative investment also buy them. A type of
corporate bond called a *convertible bond* allows the investor
to convert the bond to a prescribed number of shares of common stock in the company under specified conditions. This
offers the advantage of higher earnings if the stock goes up,
but convertible bonds have a lower yield than straight bonds.

Table 6 at the end of this chapter shows how to decipher
corporate bond quotations in newspapers.

Old stocks and bonds

So far, we've been talking about securities that are actively
traded on regional or national markets. There are other securities that are no longer actively traded that have made money
for some investors.

Perhaps you have some old stocks or bonds moldering
away in a safe deposit box or in an attic trunk. Ever wonder
whether they're worth anything? Perhaps you've even gone
so far as to ask a broker if there's still an active market for
your certificate and gotten a negative response.

Sometimes, and it's rather rare, an old certificate will
still have value because the original issuer was merged into
another company. This might have taken place years ago.

If you're curious about an old certificate, you may want to have its history traced by experts. Prudential American Securities will do the job for a fee that ranges from $20 to $30. For more information, write: Prudential American, 747 Green Street, Suite 300, Pasadena, CA 91101.

Another outfit, R. M. Smyth Company, will also trace old stocks. This company, however, has another, related line of business that might turn out to be even more interesting. Apparently, there's an active collectors' trade in old stock and bond certificates. Some old issues are worth more now as collectors' pieces than they were as active securities. For example, an old Edison Electric stock certificate with a light bulb and ancient power generation plant in its engraved vignette sells for around $175. Some old certificates personally signed by Commodore Vanderbilt (for one of his railroads) now sell for hundreds of dollars each—much more than their original value. If you're interested in this secondary collectors' market, you can get more information by writing: R. M. Smyth Company, 24 Broadway, New York, NY 10004.

Ready resources

Fail-Safe Investing (Putnam), by stock, bond, and money market expert Peter Nagan. This sensible investment book is out of print but should be available at your library. Nagan carefully and clearly describes just about every type of investment you can make. Each type of investment is explained and rated for its risk factors and tax impact.

The Power of Money Dynamics (Reston Publishers), by Venita Van Caspel, a well-known financial planner. A detailed handbook covering all facets of investing, insurance, real estate, and tax planning. For the sophisticated investor.

The Money Workbook for Women (Arbor House), by Carole Phillips, president of a financial management and consulting firm.

An excellent step-by-step guide directed toward women who have had little or no experience managing personal finances.

The Retirement Money Book (Acropolis Books), by financial planner Ferd Nauheim. Nauheim explores a variety of investment options that he recommends as particularly suitable for retired people.

Your Guide to a Financially Secure Retirement (Harper & Row), by C. Colburn Hardy, editor of the annual Dun & Bradstreet's **Guide to Your Investments.** Presents clear information on financial planning before and after retirement.

Your Retirement: A Complete Planning Guide (A&W Publishers, Inc.), by the editors of **Consumer Guide.** Covers all the financial considerations of planning for retirement.

How to Make Money in Wall Street (Doubleday), by Louis Rukeyser. Considered a classic on the stock market.

Everyone's Money Book (Delacourt Press), by Jane Bryant Quinn. An excellent money management reference book. Good choice for a home library.

Sylvia Porter's New Money Book for the 80's (Doubleday), by Sylvia Porter. Another excellent reference book for your library.

Magazines that feature money and investment-related topics and give good information in layman's language include **Money,** published monthly by Time, Inc.; and **Changing Times,** published monthly by the Kiplinger Washington Editors, Inc.

For more sophisticated investors, the following magazines offer more technical information relating to the business and financial community: **Barron's,** published weekly by Dow Jones & Co.; **Forbes,** published biweekly by Forbes, Inc.; **Fortune,** published biweekly by Time, Inc.; **Harvard Business Review,** published bimonthly by the President and Fellows of Harvard College; and **Nation's Business,** published monthly by the U.S. Chamber of Commerce.

The Wall Street Journal and the financial pages of a metropolitan newspaper are must reading for any serious investor.

Well-known syndicated newspaper columns that keep readers up to date on what's happening in the financial world include the following.

"Staying Ahead," by Jane Bryant Quinn
"Your Money's Worth," by Sylvia Porter
"How to Make Money on Wall Street," by Louis Rukeyser
"Mind Your Money," by Peter Weaver

Table 3   How to read stock quotations

"Composite" stock prices listed in newspapers are prices on sales of stocks on the day before at the New York Stock Exchange and all other exchanges combined. To read the stock table, you must decipher the headings at the top of each column.

52-week		Stock	Div.	Yld.	PE	Sales 100s	High	Low	Last	Chg.
High	Low									
15¾	5¾	AAR	.44	3.0	22	85	15¼	14¾	14¾	−¼
37¾	27½	ACF	1.40	4.1	14	181	35¾	33⅝	33⅞	−¾
20	12¼	AMF	.50	3.0	...	650	17⅛	16⅝	16¾	+⅛
35⅛	13¼	AMR Cp	...	...		2298	34⅞	34	34¾	+¼

52-week high or low	The highest and lowest price paid for the stock over the past 52 weeks. Whole numbers are expressed in dollars and fractions are expressed in cents. A high of 15¾ means $15.75, as in the first listing.
Stock	Abbreviated name of the company issuing the stock
Div.	The annual dividend the company is paying on each share
Yld.	The percentage of yield, measured by dividing the dividend by the current stock price
PE	The price-earning ratio (also referred to as the multiple); the stock's price divided by the company's yearly earnings per share of outstanding stock
Sales 100s	Number of share sales in groups of 100
High	The highest price paid for the stock that day
Low	The lowest price paid for the stock that day
Last	The last price of the day
Chg.	The change in the last price of the day compared with the day before, expressed in fractions

Table 4	How to read mutual fund quotations

	Sell	**Buy**
Acorn F	33.37	NL
ADV	22.71	NL
Afuture	18.91	NL
AIM Funds:		
CvYld	14.92	15.96
Grnwy	14.92	15.96

Mutual fund prices listed in the newspaper are always in two columns: the *sell* column and the *buy* column. These quotations are the prices at which shares in the mutual funds listed could have sold (the net asset value for each, or the prices at which an investor could sell a share back to the fund) on the previous day or could have been bought (the net value plus sales charge).

If an *NL* appears in the *buy* column, this means the fund is no-load, and the buy price will be the same as the sell price because there is no sales fee to add. Prices listed are without dollar signs. For example, in the first listing, 33.37 is $33.37 a share.

Table 5   Taxable equivalent yields

To determine yields you must earn from taxable investments to equal tax-free yields, find your taxable income and read across. The table shows approximate taxable yields that are equivalent to tax-exempt yields under current federal law for 1984. Beginning in 1985, income brackets will be indexed to reflect changes in the consumer price index.

1984 Tax year

Taxable Income (1,000's) Single Return	Joint Return	1984 Tax Bracket	Tax-free Yields 8.50%	9.00%	9.50%	10.00%	10.50%	11.00%	11.50%
$15.0–18.2		23.0%	11.04	11.69	12.34	12.99	13.64	14.29	14.94
	$24.6–29.9	25.0	11.33	12.00	12.67	13.33	14.00	14.67	15.33
18.2–23.5		26.0	11.49	12.16	12.84	13.51	14.19	14.86	15.54
	29.9–35.2	28.0	11.81	12.50	13.19	13.89	14.58	15.28	15.97
23.5–28.8		30.0	12.14	12.86	13.57	14.29	15.00	15.71	16.43
	35.2–45.8	33.0	12.69	13.43	14.19	14.93	15.67	16.42	17.16
28.8–34.1		34.0	12.88	13.64	14.39	15.15	15.91	16.67	17.42
34.1–41.5	45.8–60.0	38.0	13.71	14.52	15.32	16.13	16.94	17.74	18.55
41.5–55.3	60.0–85.6	42.0	14.66	15.52	16.38	17.24	18.10	18.97	19.83
	85.6–109.4	45.0	15.45	16.36	17.27	18.18	19.09	20.00	20.91
55.3–81.8		48.0	16.35	17.31	18.27	19.23	20.19	21.15	22.12
	109.4–162.4	49.0	16.67	17.65	18.63	19.61	20.59	21.57	22.55
Over 81.8	Over 162.4	50.0	17.00	18.00	19.00	20.00	21.00	22.00	23.00

Table 6 How to read corporate bond quotations

Only leading corporate bonds are traded on the big stock exchange boards and quoted in newspapers. Here is how to decipher the heads at the top of the columns.

			Yld.	Close	Change
AetnLf	8⅛	07	11.0	73¾	−1¼
AlaBnc	9½	84	9.58	99⅛	+⅛
AlaP	8½s	01	11.7	72⅜	...
AlaP	7⅞s	02	11.8	66⅝	+1⅛
AlaP	7¾s	02	11.9	65⅜	−⅝

Reading from left to right of the first listing:

AetnLf   Abbreviated name of the company issuing the bond

8⅛ 07   The interest rate, or coupon rate, of the bond is 8⅛ percent; maturity date is 2007

11.0   Current yield, expressing the "effective" interest rate considering the current market price of the bond (if *cv* appears in the yield column, this means that these are convertible bonds, and their yield is less important than their relationship to current stock prices)

73¾   The closing day market price, expressed as a percentage of the bond's face value; the percentage is expressed in dollars by adding a zero ($730.); any fractions in this column are figured in relation to $10—+¾, for example, means a gain of $7.50. Thus the closing day market price totals $737.50.

−1¼   The percentage in which the price at closing has dropped or increased since the previous day's closing (−$12.50)

9
U.S. government
securities

We should take a look now at the world of U.S. government securities. Along with insured savings deposits, these are the safest investments available. They don't pay the very tip-top interest rates, but you can sleep nights. Government securities carry virtually no risk.

But the word *risk* takes many forms. Sure, there's no risk to your investment principal with U.S. government offerings. They always pay the interest they say they will, and when the maturity date rolls around you always get your initial investment back.

During the period the securities are held, however, the selling price can vary. It's part of the secondary market system discussed in the section on bonds in the last chapter. As with other fixed-rate securities, if you buy a government security that's newly issued, you buy on the "primary" market. But you can also buy and sell older securities on a secondary market. A broker handles the orders. Other investors will buy your government security at a premium or at a discount, depending on what's happened to interest rates on newer issues. When interest rates go up, the price of your older fixed-rate security goes down. If you have to sell your investment before maturity, you have to sell at a discount because more recent offerings pay a better rate of return. Of course, the converse is true. If you buy a government security at $1,000, paying 10 percent, and interest rates on newer issues go down to 8 percent, the price of your investment should go up.

This bouncing around of your government security's price is not that much of a bother if the maturity date is less than a year. You won't be stuck for very long. When you start buying securities that have much longer maturity dates—two years on out to ten or twenty years—that's when you could have some serious problems with future rising interest rates and falling prices—and losses if you want to sell before maturity. To avoid the risks of investing in individual government securities, you might invest in a money market fund with a portfolio of government issues only: safe but liquid.

Having absorbed this little lecture on the machinations of the marketplace, you're ready for some details on the various types of securities the government offers and which, if any, may be right for your current or future needs.

Treasury securities

The money you earn on Treasury securities is subject to federal income tax but not state and local taxes. You can purchase U.S. Treasury offerings from a broker or bank for a fee. Or you can buy them yourself directly through an auction bidding procedure when they are issued. For information on how to purchase them yourself call or write: The Bureau of the Public Debt, Securities Transaction Branch, U.S. Treasury, Washington, DC 20226 (202) 287–4113. Or contact the Federal Reserve Bank or branch closest to you. Federal Reserve Banks or branches are located in the following major cities: Atlanta, Baltimore, Birmingham, Boston, Buffalo, Charlotte, Chicago, Cincinatti, Cleveland, Dallas, Denver, Detroit, El Paso, Helena (Montana), Houston, Jacksonville, Kansas City (Missouri), Little Rock, Los Angeles, Louisville, Memphis, Miami, Minneapolis, Nashville, New Orleans, New

York City, Oklahoma City, Omaha, Philadelphia, Pittsburgh, Portland (Oregon), Richmond, St. Louis, Salt Lake City, San Antonio, San Francisco, and Seattle.

Treasury bills
T-bills can be purchased for terms as short as thirteen weeks or twenty-six weeks. The longest term bills are for fifty-two weeks. The minimum initial investment is $10,000, and you can buy more chunks in multiples of $5,000. The interest paid closely reflects short-term interest rate fluctuations in general.

Corporations, banks, and well-heeled individual investors often "park" idle cash in Treasury bills. They get a good interest rate, if not the top rate. Their money isn't tied up in long-term obligations. And if they need quick cash for an emergency, they can sell their bills in the open market. Depending on what interest rates are doing, they make a modest profit or take a modest loss when they sell.

Treasury notes
These securities run from one to ten years. The shorter term notes, those that run from one year to three and one-half years, require a minimum investment of $5,000. All the others—on up to ten years—require a $1,000 minimum. The longer term notes are attractive to investors who want the safety of government investments but don't want to ante up the minimum $10,000 that a T-bill requires.

Treasury bonds
These long-term securities go from ten years on out to thirty, even forty years. When investors think bond interest rates are historically high, they buy in to "lock up" the rate for a long time. Sometimes they win, sometimes they lose. It's a guessing game. For example, whoever would have thought interest rates would have gone as high as 17 percent for mort-

gages and 21 percent for the prime rate (what banks charge their best business customers) back in 1981? When interest rates, in general, are that high, it kills investors who are holding older low-interest bonds.

U.S. savings bonds

You can purchase savings bonds through a bank. They are not traded on the open market like Treasury bonds. For a long time these low-cost bonds (you can buy one for as little as $25) paid scandalously low rates. Recently, they were given a shot in the arm by Congress. Now you can get new series EE bonds that pay just a shade less than five-year Treasury securities. To fully enjoy this higher rate, you've got to keep your bonds for a minimum of five years (otherwise, you get the old, lower rate). But if you do hang on for five years, you are guaranteed a minimum return of 7.5 percent.

EE bonds can be traded in at maturity for series HH bonds, thereby deferring tax owed on accumulated interest. HH bonds pay out interest on a regular basis and can be used as an income source. In general, savings bonds are not recommended as a new investment for someone who is retired. You can do better elsewhere.

But you may have amassed some older series E or H savings bonds over the years when you were working full time and are now wondering what to do with them. For information, write: U.S. Savings Bond Division, Suite 403, 1111 18th Street, N.W., Washington, DC 20226. They can also field questions about such things as lost or stolen bonds (there's a way to get your money back), and transferring ownership (to children or grandchildren).

Federal agency securities

These are investments issued by such government or government-backed organizations as The Federal Farm Credit Banks, The Federal Home Loan Mortgage Corporation

(Freddie Mac), and the Federal Small Business Administration. You buy them from a securities broker. You can purchase original issues or older issues that are sold in the marketplace.

Federal agency securities usually pay a higher interest rate than U.S. Treasury securities and are considered almost as safe. The government backs these securities one way or another, and they've never let anybody down. Some of these securities are exempt from state and local taxes; some are not. All are subject to federal income tax. The bonds, notes, and debentures are usually bought in increments of $5,000 to $10,000, but some can be purchased for as little as $1,000.

Ready resources

Handbook for Securities of the U.S. Government and Federal Agencies and Related Money Market Instruments. This long-titled tome is published every two years by the First Boston Corporation, an international banking firm headquartered in New York. For purchase information, write: First Boston Corporation, 20 Exchange Place, New York, NY 10005. Major libraries may also have copies.

Guide to Federal Agency Securities is published by the Federal Reserve Bank of New York, 33 Liberty Street, New York, NY 10045. At this writing, copies are free.

10
Life insurance, annuities, IRAs

You may wonder why life insurance is an "investment." Technically, most financial experts say, insurance is not really an investment even though it's sometimes pegged as such. Insurance salespeople may refer to their product as an "investment" because certain types of policies can build up cash values.

Many retired persons have piled up a considerable amount of cash value in their whole life, or straight life, policies that have a savings feature. (Term insurance does not have this feature.)

Because insurance may not be all that hot as an investment (it's primarily designed to protect your dependents if you die), you might want to make better use of the cash you have in your policies by investing it elsewhere to earn a higher rate of return. Traditionally, insurance companies have paid lower interest rates than you could get in the bond and money markets. This is especially true of older policies taken out back in the forties, fifties, and sixties.

Options for cash-value policies
To get started on your insurance policy analysis, get in touch with your insurance agent or the company. Ask for a statement—in writing—describing the policies you own and how much cash value, if any, you have. If you do have cash in there, here are four of your major options:

1. Surrender the policies for cash. You take out the accumulated cash and no longer have insurance coverage on your
life. This may not be a bad idea, if you've got quite a bit
of cash involved and have no immediate dependent's needs.

With a $25,000 policy that has $17,000 cash built up,
you're paying annual premiums for only $8,000 worth of
actual coverage. The $17,000 is already yours for the asking.
You can take the money and invest it in a mutual fund, a
good electric utility stock, or some other high-interest investment. Or you might want to use the money for a travel program, a boat, or whatever.

2. Get paid-up insurance. If you feel you still need a certain
amount of insurance to, say, cover a dependent spouse's needs,
you can reduce your $25,000 policy to $20,000 and be "paid
up," which means you won't have to pay any more premiums.
You can use the premium money elsewhere.

3. Reduce your coverage by half. If you'll be needing some
insurance, but not very much, you can cut your $25,000 cover-
age in half. You will have a policy with $12,500 coverage
for your beneficiaries (to cover funeral expenses, debts). And
you will have $8,500 in cash (one-half the original $17,000
cash value). This way you'll have some immediate spending
money and a modest amount of insurance to cover any beneficiary's needs.

4. Take out a loan. On some policies, especially the older
ones, you can take out low-interest (5–6 percent) loans against
your cash value. Let's say your $25,000 policy still has a
loan rate of 6 percent. You can borrow part or all of the
$17,000 cash value and invest it in something that pays as
much as 10 percent—much higher interest than what you
were getting. But be sure it's a low-risk investment. This

way, you retain a form of full protection (the remaining $8,000 insurance coverage and $17,000 invested in some "safe" security). If you do borrow, you never have to repay the loan. Annual interest can be paid and deducted from your income tax if you itemize deductions. Or you can let the insurance company add unpaid interest to your loan.

Review your options

The main idea here is to make a thorough review of your insurance needs and the investment possibilities of any cash value you might have accumulated. If you really don't need insurance, grab the cash and run. Your children may be well off on their own and your spouse may be taken care of. So why not use your cash for your own financial needs in retirement?

When you go through this review procedure, you may get a visit or letter from an insurance agent. The agent will want to go over your options in person with the idea of, perhaps, selling you something else. Take all the information and don't buy anything—no matter how appealing. Insurance agents can be powerful persuaders when it comes to converting your cash into another "product" the company sells. This could be another form of insurance ("Look, you can get twice as much coverage for the same premiums with this new, superduper XYZ policy"). Or it could be an investment in a mutual fund, annuity, or whatever.

Say you want to think it over and do just that. The insurance agent may have given good advice, and his or her "new product" may be just right for you. But how do you know? Consider the options carefully and bounce them off your tax adviser or investment adviser (if you have one). Don't be pressured into anything. You probably will be better off putting your cash into an easy-access money market account (or fund) or short-term U.S. Treasury bills.

Annuities

Having control over your money is important. This is why many retirees have resisted buying annuities offered by insurance agents, brokers, financial planners, and others. In case you didn't know, annuities are investments designed to provide a guaranteed retirement income.

With the usual annuity arrangement, called an *accumulative deferred annuity,* you pay in over a period of years and then, when you retire, you annuitize, or activate, your investment. From that day on, you get so much a month for life (and the life of your spouse if you so specify). You cannot withdraw your investment funds in a lump sum. When you die (and your spouse dies, if you have him or her covered), that's it. Any money left over in your fund goes to the insurance company.

You also can buy a *single-premium, immediate-pay annuity* with a lump sum payment. This can go into effect right away. Some retirees buy annuities with funds they have accumulated through IRAs and other pension plans. Many corporate pension plans provide payouts only in the form of an annuity—no other choice is possible.

It sounds appealing: steady, guaranteed income for life. But professional estate planners say there are some definite drawbacks. The money invested in the annuity is completely out of your control. You get the set monthly income and no more. You can't withdraw extra funds if there's an emergency or if you want to use the money elsewhere.

There are at least thirty different ways annuities can be written. You can work it so your beneficiaries can get some money if you die before a specified date. With a *joint-survivorship* annuity, your spouse will get money after you die (it probably will be a reduced amount).

You can buy a *period-certain* annuity which pays an agreed-upon amount of money for a specified number of years. You can pick these terms for up to ten years or more. With a ten-year annuity, all your funds are supposed to be paid out during that period. If you die in, say, six years, your spouse or other beneficiaries will get the remainder of the money paid out over the remaining four years (or, if specified, they could get the remainder in a lump sum).

You can check the financial stability of companies that sell annuities in a reference book called *Bests' Insurance Reports,* which may be available at your local library. Companies are rated from A-plus to C, depending upon their ability to manage well despite recessions or other adverse developments.

IRAs (Individual Retirement Accounts)

An IRA is a tax shelter for earned income. Whatever earned salary, wages, or commissions up to $2,000 yearly (plus an additional $250 for a dependent spouse) you place in an IRA is deductible from the taxable income you report to the IRS. Your money plus whatever your money earns while it's sheltered in the IRA is free from taxes until you withdraw it.

An IRA is often described as the perfect retirement investment plan. Unfortunately, IRAs arrived too late on the scene to benefit most people already retired or reaching retirement age today. But, if you are younger than age 70½ and are still working, you may get some tax benefits from an IRA.

You can establish an IRA with any qualified custodian of IRAs, such as a financial institution, money market fund, brokerage firm, insurance company, or mutual fund. This means that you can choose from a variety of investment vehicles: e.g., CDs, money market fund shares, stocks, bonds. Government regulations allow you to switch your IRA to another custodian—another firm—without penalty once a year. You can change the type of investments for your IRA as often as you like so long as the custodian remains the same.

You *must* start taking money out from an IRA by age 70½ or there is a heavy penalty. Before this age, you must set up a system of withdrawal that will reduce the amount of funds in your IRA to zero within your life expectancy as shown by annuity tables in the IRS publication #575, *Pension and Annuity Income.*

An excellent guide to evaluating different IRAs is *The IRA Book,* by Robert Krughoff and the staff of the Center for the Study of Services, 1518 K Street, N.W., Suite 406, Washington, DC 20005. Available for $5.95 from the Center.

Pension payout options

If you have a large sum of money coming to you from a pension or profit-sharing plan, and if you have a choice as to payouts, there are other payout possibilities besides an annuity you should investigate. You might have your employer pay you in installments over X number of years. The advantage to this is that your heirs can have the remainder of the money if you die before the installment period is up. The disadvantage is that the installments will be taxed the full amount as ordinary income (except for the money you contributed).

You can take your lump sum and pay a relatively light tax (on the part your employer contributed) based on a complicated ten-year income averaging procedure. It's an excellent tax break and should be investigated.

You can also place your lump sum payment into a special rollover IRA which will defer taxes until you start to withdraw money. (At age 70½, the law says, you have to start withdrawing IRA funds.) This rollover IRA can be used only for this purpose. You cannot add funds.

You have an option with an IRA rollover. You can put in the whole lump sum you get from your pension or profit sharing plan. Or you can put in part of the money. This way you can use some of the money now (and pay tax on it) and put the rest away for a rainy day—tax deferred.

Any time you have a sizable amount of money coming to you from a pension plan, get advice from a tax professional. Too much is at stake to fumble this close to the goal line.

11
The risky routes

Having covered some "safe" investments, we're ready to take a look at speculative, high-risk investments. Some people have made lots of money with speculative ventures. They're the ones the salespeople are always telling you about. But the vast majority of investors who buy heavily into such things as gold or collectibles get burned.

Precious metals and gems

These "sure" investments were supposed to be a perfect hedge against the raging inflation of the early eighties. They were also supposed to be a hedge against such fearful possibilities as "the complete collapse of our monetary system," and "political chaos." If you hoarded gold or diamonds, so the theory went, you would have wealth when everyone else was out in the street begging or looting.

Sounds a bit silly, but many a novice investor fell for the scare tactic and bought precious metals and gems as hedges and/or as potential big profit makers. Unfortunately, some brokers and financial planners—who should have known better—got their customers into one bad investment after another. Later on, when these poor clients wanted to get their money out, they could do so only at considerable loss. The speculative, puffed-up market finally collapsed.

To repeat some wisdom you may have absorbed earlier on in this book: Don't invest in anything you don't understand. If you're an expert on precious metals and gems, you're not concerned with this section. Move on. If you're not an expert, maybe you should stay out of the game entirely.

There is a way into the contest through the back door which just might be pleasing and profitable for investors who take some time to do a little comparison shopping. If you have extra money (money you don't need for your financial future), you may want to buy antique jewelry or other objets d'art for the pure pleasure of it. There are some relative bargains to be had in this field. Buy fine workmanship and years later your purchase will not only have held its value, it also may have appreciated in value. It could be something worthwhile to leave for your heirs, give to a dear friend or family member while you're alive, or sell at a profit.

The dream of buying precious metals and gems as pure "investments" dies hard, though. Perhaps you need some convincing. Listen to financial expert Peter Nagan in his book *Fail-Safe Investing* (Putnam):

"If you think that the world is going to pieces in a hurry, then you may feel more comfortable owning gold. . . . But there are those who wonder whether, in an anarchic world, you'll be allowed to keep your gold, once you take it out of the vault and try to spend it. Won't the lawless take it by brute force?"

Many commodities experts feel that as a hedge against inflation, gold has lost its glitter. Its price has already risen so high and come down so low, its future is too risky to predict. The same thing, to varying degrees, holds true for silver, platinum, and so-called investment diamonds. Silver was pumped up to around $50 an ounce and then crashed back to the $5 level. It has come up some since, but not all that much. "Investment" diamonds (supposedly the brightest and least flawed) at one stage of the madness were selling for around $60,000 a carat. Now, they're difficult to unload at $17,000 a carat.

If you're set on investing in gems or gold, follow the guidelines outlined in the next sections. Keep in mind that these investments pay no interest or dividends and are expensive to keep (insurance, storage costs).

Buying gems as an investment

Before you buy any gem as an investment obtain several price quotes. A stone you buy should have a recent certificate of quality—from the U.S. Gemological Services for rubies, emeralds, or sapphires and from the Gemological Institute of America for diamonds. It's also a good idea to have the gem analyzed by a bonded and insured gem laboratory, which will guarantee accuracy by international standards. Some gem dealers will offer an unconditional guarantee to repurchase the gems you buy if you're not satisfied.

Diamond jewelry A diamond in a jewelry setting, given with love for an anniversary or just for the fun of it, continues to be a popular "investment." Love continues unabated while inflation and political upheaval ebb and flow. If you buy diamond jewelry, keep in mind that you will be buying at the retail price, but if you want to sell, you usually will have to sell at wholesale. To get the best buy for your money at retail, shop around among the best-established, independent jewelers and look for beauty and workmanship. Compare size and weight (carat) and how the diamond looks. Price is not necessarily a good guide to value.

Buying gold as an investment

If you want to have some gold in your investment portfolio, for the long haul, your best bet is a gold bullion "investment" coin such as the South African Krugerrand, Canadian Mapleleaf, or the new U.S. coin. Coin dealers (usually listed in the phone book Yellow Pages) buy and sell these gold pieces at prices that are pegged to daily quotes from the international gold exchanges in New York and London. Some banks, international trading companies, and brokers also sell gold coins.

Gold bullion is also sold in the form of wafers and bars of various sizes. Small bars (several ounces up to about two pounds) are sold through coin dealers and brokerage houses. Larger bars are available through gold dealers, refiners, some brokerage houses, and banks. A disadvantage of large bars is that they can't be broken down easily into small amounts if you want to sell a fraction of your holdings. Also, bars are more easily counterfeited than coins, and you might have to pay for a metal test costing as much as $75 a bar when you want to sell them. If you buy gold bullion, you should insure it and rent a safe deposit box for safekeeping.

Gold stocks and gold stock mutual funds offer a way to invest in gold and gain a dividend on your investment. Like all other stocks, stocks of gold mining companies are tied to the performance of the company. Buying gold stocks through a mutual fund is less risky than buying individual stocks, as the investment risk is spread among various gold mining companies.

Commodities futures

From time to time, brokers, financial planners, or others may try to interest clients in buying commodities futures. If carefully researched, with carefully timed purchases, commodities futures can make money for you. But, you have to become an expert in the supply and demand dynamics of the commodities markets.

Commodities as an investment involves pledging a certain price now for a particular commodity (e.g., wheat, cattle, foreign currency, metals) that will not be sold until some time later. In effect you are gambling that the future price will be higher than what you pledge now. If the future price turns out to be less, you've lost the gamble and must take a loss. Different kinds of futures are traded on different boards of exchanges, such as the Chicago Board of Trade and the New York Cotton Exchange.

Commodities are volatile and speculative investments. Be wary of any investment adviser or service that recommends commodities as a "sure thing." Some retired persons have had their savings wiped out by ill-advised plunges in the commodities markets. It's a wild and woolly game for the experts.

Collectibles

For a while, in the late seventies and early eighties, collectibles became a form of speculative commodity. Ordinarily sensible people rushed out to buy high-priced Tiffany lamps, paintings, antiques, limited-edition plates, medallions, whatever. Then the bottom fell out. A year or so later, you could buy the same items at auction for almost half price. That's when bargain hunters (expert buyers) swooped in to help the hapless unload.

Collectibles are fine, if you're a true collector or at least someone who has studied the market and knows values. But unless you get great pleasure out of such things as stamps or rare coins—and you can well afford them—they're best left to experts. The best collectible investments are often practical items you can use in your home, such as antique furniture.

Antique furniture

If you have $1,000 or so to spend, you can find some good investment buys in the field of antique furniture. An astute buyer can get beautiful, well-made, useful furnishings for the home that will increase in value.

If you bought a new, top-of-the-line piece of living-room furniture, its value would probably drop over the years. If you spent the same money, or slightly more, on a similar antique piece, its value should increase over the years. A good investment? Yes. But you didn't plan it that way. You bought the piece for its beauty and its usefulness.

You can buy good antiques from well-established dealers and from an increasing number of department stores. The pieces are usually certified and in excellent condition. But you pay the full retail price. Dealers and store managers have to mark up their antique purchases at least 80 to 100 percent to cover overhead costs. You might find better prices in some of the big department stores because they don't have the overhead of an antique shop. They have a diversity of things to sell and don't depend on the sale of antiques for all their profits.

But the best deal in antique furniture (antique anything, for that matter) may be the full-scale professional auction. Major metropolitan areas usually have at least one or two well-established auction houses.

How do you know how much to bid at an auction? You've got to learn the game—and learn values. Do a lot of shopping around antique stores for the kind of item you need. Begin to see what you can get for how much. Then, attend several auctions. Look at the goods beforehand (they usually let you inspect the items a day or two in advance). Write down imaginary bid limits for the items you like. Get a feel of how prices go.

When you bid at an auction, you're going against professionals who are dealers, you're going against an occasional professional decorator and, of course, you're going against people such as yourself—educated amateurs (let's hope you're educated). Since a dealer has to make around 100 percent on a mark-up, you can generally bid a little above his or her top limit.

As you can see, purchasing useful antiques takes time and patience. But for some retirees it can be lots of fun and, perhaps, profitable.

So far, we've been talking mainly about tangible—easy-to-see, easy-to-touch—risky investments. You can also invest in less tangible risky investments such as a franchised business.

Franchises

With a franchise you buy the know-how, a territory, and some inventory. A sort of "instant" business. Franchises can be profitable. They can also be disasters.

Obviously, if you know all about the fast food business or the motel business, you can make a lot of money with a hamburger place or a motor lodge. That's the big time— and it's a lot of hard work. You're retired, remember? The big-time franchisors don't want you unless you've got experience in the field, some working capital, and the capacity to work, work, work.

What we're talking about here is not the big time. It's the fly-by-night franchisors who want your money and don't care whether you sell any of the product or service. These companies employ the "make big money" and "no experience necessary" ads. Some just want to unload low-quality inventory at high prices. They give you a "manual for success" and then get you to buy up a basement full of the current junk they're peddling.

Don't ever invest one cent in a franchise deal until you and your lawyer and your accountant and other professionals have checked out the field of interest and the local business possibilities. If possible, work in the field (at someone else's establishment) for a while to see how the business goes and whether you really like this sort of thing.

Having taken a crack at the fly-by-night franchises, we should emphasize that quite a few small franchise operations are legitimate opportunities for those investors who want to put in the research time and the work time.

For more information about franchises, write: International Franchise Association, Suite 1005, 1025 Connecticut Avenue, N.W., Washington, DC 20036.

Direct sales companies

In a somewhat related field, you might be better off investigating the possibility of working as an independent contractor for a company that specializes in person-to-person, neighborhood sales. Most of these major manufacturing and marketing companies are members of the Direct Selling Association, 1730 M Street, N.W., Suite 610, Washington, DC 20036. If you send in a letter requesting information on how to get in touch with the various direct sales companies, you'll get a directory with more than 100 names, addresses, and descriptions of products. You can also request a booklet describing the Association's code of ethics and recent tax information concerning the establishment of a small business at home.

If you like selling and are enthusiastic about a certain type of product, you may be successful with this kind of business. As a rule, you'll never get stuck with a lot of inventory you can't return, and you'll be working with some of the top companies in the field.

More often than not, sales are conducted through in-home parties. You show off your wares to a bunch of neighbors invited in for coffee or tea by a neighborhood hostess or host. If you are handy at making your own products, such as jewelry, quilts, leather products, or whatever, you might be able to include them along with the big-name product you're selling.

Terrific deals

When you deal with companies that are members of the International Franchise Association or the Direct Selling Association, you're dealing with well-established organizations that have reputations to maintain. They have ethical codes and can discipline members on the rare occasion that this might be necessary.

But there are legions of other, smaller organizations that fall into the fly-by-night category. Some are outright crooks. Some are just inept dreamers who go bankrupt and leave you in the lurch.

"Make money at home." You've seen the ads. You

send in money and are supposedly given the "key to success." Usually, you're asked for more money. The U.S. Postal Service is constantly going after unscrupulous mail-order outfits who sell make-money-at-home schemes. You are told you can make $10,000 a year by just sitting home making phone calls or stuffing envelopes. You pay good money for the "secret to success" and get a tired list of companies that don't want your services.

Watch out for any proposals—in ads, on the telephone, in letters, or in person—that bring to mind the phrase "too good to be true." Home businesses, real estate riches, diamonds, oil bonanzas are sometimes touted that way.

Whenever a "terrific deal" is touted by an ebullient salesperson, get it down in writing and have it checked by a lawyer or accountant, or both, before you invest a dime. Check out any business proposal with others in the trade.

Limited partnerships

Stay away from poorly managed limited partnerships with a small, "select" group participating (if you're lucky, they say, you can still get in). The idea may be okay, but the management and the timing may be way off.

On the other hand, a well-chosen limited partnership investment sponsored by a company with a good track record can be a good way to make money and cut your tax bill (if you're in a high tax bracket) at the same time. There are two basic kinds of limited partnerships—public and private.

The public offerings, which are sold by stockbrokers and financial planners, must follow marketing guidelines set out by the Securities and Exchange Commission.

Private offerings have fewer shares for sale and less regulation by the SEC. These investments are riskier and should be avoided unless you have a good line on the history and performance of the offering company.

Some limited partnerships are purchased primarily for

the tax deductions they can provide (depreciation deductions, start-up losses, and the like). Others can be purchased for income with less emphasis on tax breaks.

Real estate partnerships offered by well-established companies may be your best bet. Oil and gas drilling partnerships are riskier, and partnerships involved in the leasing of equipment can tie your money up for many years. All limited partnerships usually lock in your money for at least five years.

Ready resources

Franchise and Business Opportunities. For a free copy of this very informative booklet on franchises, write: Franchise Department, Federal Trade Commission, 600 E Street, N.W., Washington, DC 20580.

How to Spot a Con Artist is a booklet published by AARP with a grant from the Law Enforcement Assistance Administration, U.S. Department of Justice. Write: AARP, 1909 K Street, N.W., Washington, DC 20049.

12
How about working?

In previous chapters, we talked about all sorts of investments—savings accounts, securities, and the like. We ended
up with a look into investments that require some work as
well as some money (franchises and direct sales contracts).
Now, we're going to investigate the ultimate investment, the
one that requires your time and brainpower but not necessarily your money.

Your best investment
We rarely look at ourselves as having our own intrinsic investment potential. Yet, we have the ability to make more money
with our own brains and bodies than with all other kinds
of investments combined. We may not choose to do so, but
we have the potential.

We're not talking about *going back to work.* You're
retired and you probably like the easier pace. But if you
could be persuaded to do something you really get a kick
out of, part time, and get paid for your efforts, wouldn't
you seriously consider the possibility?

Some people take to retirement very well. They like
the freedom, the extra time, and the lack of pressure. They
have things to do, trips to take, books to read.

Others are satisfied with this routine for a while and
then things begin to pall. They become bored. They feel that
the other world—people who are working full time—looks
at them as second-class citizens who are "over the hill."

And, for a growing number of retirees, there's another

nagging problem: Money. Their Social Security and small pension or modest investments are not adding up right. They have less and less to spend. Inflation has jacked up prices to the point where the planned retirement money is not stretching enough to cover those retirement dreams.

If someone came along and said you could have extra income to cover many, if not all, of your retirement dreams, you'd jump at the chance. Right? Well settle back and keep an open mind. We're going to suggest the possibility of putting yourself to work at something you like to do.

First, a little arithmetic. Let's say you are getting $8,000 a year, tax free, from Social Security. Let's also say you are getting $6,000 a year from a pension plan and/or from various investments. You've got $14,000 coming in every year and that's not too bad because the bulk of it is tax free. Nevertheless, $14,000 may not allow some of your big retirement dreams to be realized. When you start traveling or investing in a camper—whoosh goes the money.

Let's say you can make $5.00 an hour at a leisurely pace (20 hours a week) doing some sort of activity that's psychologically and financially rewarding. This is within the bounds of reasonable expectations.

Working an average of 20 hours a week will give you around $6,000 a year. This amount of money is within the $6,600 (1983) earned income limit for Social Security for people aged 65 to 70. There is no limit for people over age 70. For people under 65 the limit is $4,920 (1983). You can take in your $6,000 and still continue to get full Social Security benefits—no penalties. A couple, with both partners working at part-time jobs, can easily get double $6,000—up to $13,000-plus—without losing a penny of Social Security benefits. Three Social Security pamphlets—*How Work Affects Your Social Security Check, If You're Self-Employed,* and *Reporting Your Income for Social Security*—give full details. The pamphlets are available at your local Social Security office.

In the example we're examining, you add the new

earned income to your existing $14,000 and you get a nice $20,000 annual total. You now have considerably more money to do the things you listed in your retirement goal plan. As a dividend, you'll probably be out and around more, meeting new people and, quite possibly, enjoying better health. Remember, the more money you can drum up on your own, the longer you can leave your basic capital investments alone. In a sense, you'll be working for more current income and for capital preservation.

The case for older workers

If you're worried about not doing a good job because of your age, relax. You have a lot to offer. Age is simply not a good criteria for determining an individual's ability to handle a job.

J. Myron Johnson, professor of industrial psychology, Stevens Institute of Technology, writing in the *Harvard Business Review,* says, "From a work capability viewpoint, the greatest physical decline occurs in the late thirties and early forties with later physical decline not having a great deal of occupational significance."

There are all sorts of reports and studies floating around that show how older workers can compete handily with younger workers. What the older worker may lose in speed and stamina, he or she gains with experience, motivation, and reliability.

Listen to what these employers in the Chicago area say about older workers they've hired through project ABLE (Ability Based on Long Experience) in the booklet *Employers Speak Out:*

Insurance company: "They (older workers) have demonstrated their ability to take on new tasks and impart their knowledge to others."

Major bank: "Their turnover rate is 5 percent compared with 20 percent for the younger pool of workers. . . . Older workers provide good role models."

Florist chain: "Older workers can adapt more easily to nonstandard schedules than younger workers."

Are you hearing what these employers are saying? They're giving you clever clues as to how to market yourself in the employment world. What you've got to sell is your experience, motivation, and reliability. You may even have some special skills. All this adds up to an attractive package for knowledgeable employers. Many younger workers can't match it.

Strategically, you're more flexible than a younger worker. You don't have to work to support a young family. You're not hell bent on climbing the ladder. You have no special image to maintain in an organization.

Banks, insurance companies, and other financial organizations that have backlogs of office work piled up are often willing to hire older workers because of their reliability and their flexibility. Financial organizations have shown a lot less inclination than other businesses to discriminate against job applicants because of their age.

Recent age-discrimination court judgments have made believers out of a growing number of employers. An amendment to the Age Discrimination in Employment Act (ADEA) went into effect in 1979. This amendment says you can't be turned down for a job, passed by for promotion, fired, be forced to retire, or be denied training because of your age prior to age 70. For more information write: Equal Employment Opportunity Commission, Office of Public Affairs, 2401 E Street, N.W., Room 4202, Washington, DC 20506. (If you have a complaint, contact: EEOC, 1717 H Street, N.W., Suite 400, Washington, DC 20506; 202–653–6197.)

Make a skills inventory

To get started in a job search, take an inventory of your skills and predilections. Maybe some hobby or line of work way back when can be summoned forth to help with today's employment search. You might have been an outstanding cook and "purchasing agent" for a large family. Why not put these skills and experience to work in a small restaurant, inn, or country club?

If you are good at tennis, golf, boating, skiing, music, whatever, you might be able to do repair work, give lessons, or sell equipment. You're already ahead of most job applicants. You're an expert. An employer doesn't have to spend a lot of time and money training you.

Try a temporary employment agency

Maybe it's been a long time since you've gone out to look for a job. You may be out of practice. One way to get started, to get an idea of what's available and what's being paid, is to sign up with a temporary agency. Temporary agencies are listed in the phone book Yellow Pages.

As a temporary, you're on call and when something comes up you're rented out to a client. You move around to interesting places and rarely have enough time at any one job to become bored. A good way to check out the job market and get paid while you're doing it.

You may also want to use special employment agencies designed to help "over-60" workers get back into part-time (even full-time) jobs.

Read guides to getting a job

According to John Truitt, author of *Telesearch: Direct Dial the Best Job of Your Life,* a telephone could be the best job-search tool available. You use the phone to line up interviews, and interviews are what it's all about.

Telesearch is an excellent guide to getting a job—for people of all ages. It's published by Facts on File, 460 Park Avenue South, New York, NY 10016.

Incidentally, the phone book Yellow Pages can serve as a handy job locater. Potential employers are listed according to subject ("Accountants" to "Zipper Repairing"). You get addresses, phone numbers—everything neat and tidy.

Other good reading on how to get a job: Richard La-throp's *Who's Hiring Who*, published by Ten Speed Press, Box 7123, Berkeley, CA 94707 (if you can't find it in your local library or book store). Lathrop shows how to market yourself—at any age. You are told how to prepare a "Qualifications Brief" instead of the old-fashioned resume routine.

Use volunteer work as a stepping-stone

Another possible way into the world of work is the volunteer field. Perhaps you've already been a candy-striper at a hospital or a faithful fundraiser for organizations. But this is not what we're talking about.

It's entirely possible to use a top-notch volunteer job as a training station for a paid job later on. Through a carefully selected volunteer job you can learn more about your field of interest (medicine, education, administration, counseling). You can become a semipro in your selected field. And you can meet potential employer contacts on the outside.

Example: A retired schoolteacher in the Boston area went to work as a volunteer for a small hospital to help develop a training course for volunteers (candy-stripers, book mobile, gift shop). She did an excellent job, which was noticed by the personnel chief of a major hospital in the area. The "retired" teacher was offered a paid position to set up a training program for nurses and lab technicians as well as volunteers. At thirty hours a week for good pay she had the best of both worlds—extra income and plenty of time for leisure activities.

When you look for a volunteer job, take plenty of care in the procedure—same as you would for a paid job. Talk to the Voluntary Action Center in your area (United Way and other charities should know the phone number).

You might also want to check out the volunteer job-search book *On Your Way: A Workbook for Volunteers and Interns.* It shows how to select the field that's best for you and how to find a volunteer job that can lead to paid employment. For more information, write: Career and Voluntary Advisory Service, Civic Center and Clearinghouse, Inc., 14 Beacon Street, Boston, MA 02100.

When you apply for a volunteer job, be sure to ask for a written job description (the more professional sounding the better) that outlines your duties, training, responsibilities, and hours (these are often quite flexible).

Start a home business

Then there's the whole area of starting up your own small business at home. If you can pull this off, you've got several things going your way: (1) you get double duty out of your home—as a shelter and as a low-overhead work site; (2) you can work at your own pace in the way that suits you best; (3) if you're married, you and your spouse can work together; and (4) you can get some nifty deductions to reduce the income tax bite.

Right now, more than five million Americans are working full time at home making money with home businesses. This population could grow to fifteen million during the eighties as the home computer and electronics communication fields continue to expand.

A retired person with a computer hookup at home can (with training) do word processing and programming chores for a single employer or a list of client companies. Home computers can be easily connected to a big computer network through a "modem" telephone coupling device. You can do your work, send it in, and pass messages back and forth through your computer connection. One thing to think about with a home computer hookup: isolation. You don't get to commune with colleagues—except through the video message system.

Some home computer buffs, who don't mind momentary isolation, are selling their own electronic newsletters and consulting services over network connections. The Source, a computer "utility" service owned by the *Reader's Digest,* offers subscribers all sorts of useful programs. To name a few: electronic newsletter "publishing," electronic bulletin boards for the sale or purchase of almost anything you can think of, and access to stock market analysis reports and packaged information sources. For more details write: Source Telecommunications, 1616 Anderson Road, McLean, VA 22012.

The entire home business area, including the burgeoning computer field, is on the move. To find out what's happening around the country, write: The National Association for The Cottage Industry, 1206 West Webster Street, Chicago, IL 60614. You can subscribe to their newsletter, *Mind Your Own Business,* which describes other small businesses that have been successful and provides tips on taxes, advertising, accounting, and business management.

Tax deductions

At least a little part of the fun of working at home is the potential tax advantage you can get. You can use an entire room or part of a room and deduct the cost of cleaning, heating, air conditioning, and depreciation (this is a big one). The equipment you buy can initially qualify for money-saving investment tax credits and you can write off the equipment with annual depreciation deductions (recently sweetened up by Congress).

You need the advice of a good tax accountant because deductions for a business in your home are subject to strict interpretation of the rules, which may limit the amount of tax you can write off. Also, you can't possibly know all the available deductions and you may run into trouble if you want to sell your home in the near future (you might have to pay a special tax on that depreciated work space). Check out the Internal Revenue Service publication #587, *Business Use of Your Home.*

Homeowners insurance

If you do start a business at home, be sure to check how this might affect the coverage on your homeowners policy. In many cases, liability coverage is not valid with a home business, for example. You may have to obtain a different type of policy.

Ready resources

Second Career Opportunities for Older Persons. This free AARP booklet covers an array of agencies and organizations designed to help older workers. Lots of source names and addresses. Write: AARP, 1909 K Street, N.W., Washington, DC 20049.

Volunteer organizations

ACTION, 806 Connecticut Avenue, N.W., Washington, DC 20525. Administers Peace Corps, VISTA, RSVP, Foster Grandparents, and Senior Companions programs.

Big Brothers/Big Sisters Association of America, 117 S. 17th Street, Philadelphia, PA 19103.

Literacy Volunteers of America, 700 E. Water Street, Syracuse, NY 13210.

Volunteer: The National Center for Citizen Involvement, 1214 16th Street, N.W., Washington, DC 20036. A clearinghouse of information on volunteer programs throughout the country.

National Park Service, Room 1013, Washington, DC 20240. Ask for brochure on volunteering in national parks. Or write your regional office of the National Park Service.

National School Volunteer Program, 300 N. Washington Street, Alexandria, VA 22314. Write for information on how to start or join a school volunteer program.

Small Business Administration, 1441 L Street, N.W., Washington, DC 20414. Offers many publications on starting and running your own business—for novice and veteran business owners. Oversees SCORE and ACE programs, for which retired businessmen may volunteer their services for people who need advice or help with their small businesses. Check your local SBA office also.

Lightbulb magazine. Inventors Workshop International publishes this handy guide for budding inventors. If you become a member of IWI, you get help with sorting out patent possibilities—from inception on through the patent search, technical details, and final patent application. For more information, write: Inventors Workshop International, 1781 Callens Road, Ventura, CA 93003.

How to Start Your Own Business and Succeed. Published by McGraw-Hill, this book is for serious self-bossers (got the idea and are ready to go). Written by Arthur H. Kuriloff, a small business management specialist, and John M. Hemphill, Jr., Associate Dean of the School of Business Management, UCLA. You learn about all phases of management and marketing.

How to Form Your Own Corporation Without a Lawyer, written by Ted Nicholas, published by Enterprise Publishing Co., 501 Beneficial Building, Wilmington, DE 19801. Outlines potential tax breaks.

13
Your health

This part of the book is devoted to areas where you may be able to cut your basic expenses without cutting too much, if anything, out of your retirement goals. By dealing successfully with the demand side items on your balance sheet, you should be able to, indeed, "live better for less."

In this chapter, we'll take a look at your health. Why is this subject included in a book that deals with financial planning? Because many people spend a lot of money on their health care. This is especially true after they reach 65 and beyond.

There are two basic ways to cut your health care costs: (1) give yourself better odds for better health by practicing "preventive medicine" in your daily life, and (2) form an active partnership with a "good" primary-care physician who will help you obtain maximal coverage for medical services from Medicare and supplemental health insurance.

Practice preventive medicine
Proper exercise and diet and periodic physical checkups will help you maintain a good overall wellness quotient. An ounce of prevention is always worth a pound of cure—especially when the cost per pound is so high.

Exercise
You should take on some form of regular exercise, if you've not already done so, even if you're way out of shape or

have medical conditions that lead you to consider yourself somewhat fragile. Of course, you should check with your doctor before you take on anything strenuous.

Regular exercise can do a lot for you. One study after another has shown that specific exercises are beneficial and even essential for one's ability to function well in daily life. What kind of exercises should you do? Fitness experts agree that ideally everyone, including older people, should do some kind of sustained vigorous aerobic ("with oxygen") exercise such as brisk walking to benefit the heart, lungs, and blood vessels and to alleviate stress, some kind of exercises such as calisthenics to strengthen the muscles, and some kind of stretching exercises to improve flexibility and joint mobility and to prevent or relieve aches and pains.

How often should you exercise? According to Dr. Herbert A. de Vries, director of the physiology of exercise laboratory at the Andrus Gerontology Center, "Research has shown that older persons need exercise only three to five times a week for a minimum of twenty minutes a session to maintain fitness."

De Vries and other fitness experts recommend tailoring your own exercise routine to fit your state of health and fitness. A typical low-intensity exercise session for a previously sedentary older person might begin with "warm-up" stretching exercises, followed by a period of sustained walking, then a brief calisthenics routine, and end with "cooldown" stretching exercises. As someone improves in fitness, he or she can gradually work up into more vigorous walking, perhaps walking/jogging or running to get a greater aerobic action going, and even sports.

If you are restricted in mobility, you can do special bed, chair, and/or standing exercises (outlined in many sources) that will help you feel better and function better every day.

There are many good exercise books and booklets that

you can follow to develop your own basic routine. Three that you might consider are *Fitness after 50* (Charles Scribner's Sons, 1982), by Herbert de Vries with Dianne Hales; *Sixty-Plus & Fit Again: Exercises for Older Men and Women* (M. Evans, 1977), by Magda Rosenberg; and *Be Alive as Long as You Live* (Preventicare Publications, 1980), by Lawrence J. Frankel and Betty Byrd Richard. *Fitness Challenge of the Later Years* is a good pamphlet available for a slight charge from the Superintendent of Documents, U.S. Government Printing Office, Washington, DC 20402. *Dynamic Fitness* is a guidebook available for $.50 postage and handling charge from Action for Independent Maturity, a division of AARP. Write: AIM Guidebooks, P.O. Box 2240, Long Beach, CA 90801.

Many senior centers and adult education facilities offer exercise classes for seniors. Joining a class is always a good way to keep yourself on a regular exercise timetable.

Daily diet

Just as important as exercise is your daily diet. You may have settled into a food pattern that suited you well when you were younger. Now it may be inappropriate. As you grow older, you require less food energy (and fewer calories) because the aging body has fewer cells and demands less upkeep. This means that if you continue to eat the calorie-laden foods you ate when you were younger, even if they're smaller portions, your body stores the extra calories as fat instead of burning them up for energy. (This is another good reason for exercising. The metabolic rate is raised for more than six hours after exercise so that your body continues to consume more calories after as well as during exercise. And exercise increases appetite only when done for more than an hour a day.)

Aside from the calorie/fat question, you need to look at the issue of "empty" calories. Because you usually eat smaller portions of food now than when you were younger, you may not be getting enough nutrients in your daily diet if you concentrate on foods that are high in calories but low in nutritive value. Also, if you are taking any kind of medications, these may interfere with absorption of nutrients by the body.

Good guidelines to follow are those provided in the pamphlet *Nutrition and Your Health: Dietary Guidelines for Americans,* U.S. Department of Agriculture/Health, Education and Welfare, 1980. In brief, cut down on fatty foods; reduce sugar, salt, and caffeine. Eat more fruits, vegetables, and whole grains to increase complex carbohydrate consumption. Eat less red meat, butter, and eggs and more poultry and fish to lower cholesterol intake.

Your local heart association, university agricultural extension service, and your Area Agency on Aging all should have basic nutritious diet plans you can follow. Stay away from fad diets and very-low-in-calories diet plans—these can produce permanent harmful effects on bodily functioning.

Alcohol and smoking Some authorities say that alcohol taken in moderation (a glass of wine a day) is good for you at this stage. Underline that word *moderation.* But alcohol can be very dangerous when mixed with medications, and since many older people are on medications, alcohol cannot be routinely recommended. Of course, the dangers of excessive alcohol are well known, as are the dangers of smoking. Smoking anything is out. If you need help in breaking the habit, enroll in a "stop smoking" course at your local hospital. You're never too old to quit.

Drugs If you take medications of any kind, ask your doctor to explain possible harmful interactions of a particular drug with other drugs and with food.

Physical checkups

Like machinery, the human body needs a checkup now and then. There's a certain amount of controversy swirling around the question of whether large-scale annual physical checkups are necessary. Most doctors do agree that certain bodily functions and organs should be checked periodically.

Blood pressure is an obvious item, and it's easy to check. You can buy simple equipment to take your own blood pressure at home in between doctor's checkups. Communities often sponsor free blood pressure testing at intervals throughout the year at senior centers or other locations.

Older men should have the prostate gland checked once a year or so. Women should have a periodic Pap test (for possible cancer of the cervix) and should learn how to check their breasts for suspicious lumps that may mean cancer.

Your blood chemistry should be tested from time to time. This is especially important for people who may be having problems with elevated blood cholesterol. A simple urine test can indicate whether one might be a candidate for diabetes. And now there's a simple home test for detecting early signs of cancer—you mail a paper-smear stool sample in and it's analyzed to reveal whether there's any blood in the intestines (early warning for cancer).

Some doctors may want you to have an occasional electrocardiogram and a proctoscopic exam of the anus, rectum, and colon every two or three years. Eyes should be checked annually with a tonometry test for glaucoma.

Routine checkups can play an important part in preventive health care. Unfortunately, many people avoid routine exams because Medicare and private health insurance policies do not pay the costs of routine doctor's services and tests that are not specifically diagnostic of illness—i.e., that are not pre-hospitalization tests. Cost is a problem. One way to cut the costs of routine checkups and tests is to take advantage of any free health testing services provided by communities or local hospitals to seniors. Another way may be to enroll in a Health Maintenance Organization.

Health Maintenance Organizations (HMOs)

An HMO may provide the kind of comprehensive coverage of health-care services that retired persons require. An advantage with an HMO is that all health services, even routine checkups, are provided for through the organization's staff of doctors and other medical professionals and facilities when you pay the established monthly premium. Because routine visits are paid for, participants are more likely to seek medical attention before illnesses become serious. HMOs are establishing a good record for preventive medicine and health care.

If you enroll in an HMO, your membership takes the place of supplementary health insurance—the membership *is* your insurance. Owing to the ability of HMOs to limit hospitalization in many instances, HMO's premiums seem to increase more slowly than other comparable forms of health insurance coverage.

There are some drawbacks to HMOs. If you travel, your HMO membership may offer limited coverage for medical services you may require at some out-of-town hospital or doctor's office. Many HMOs are not geared to caring for older people's specific needs—there simply are not a lot of older people in HMOs. Some HMOs are reluctant to accept Medicare enrollees (although many are geared to operate in cooperation with Medicare). One disadvantage that should not be overlooked is that enrolling in an HMO probably will disrupt or terminate any previous relationship you've had with a primary-care doctor. The HMO pays only for the services of doctors on the staff of the HMO. If you have confidence in your present doctor, don't disrupt this relationship without some very serious thought first.

Your local Social Security office can advise you about

HMOs in your area. You can also inquire at your state insurance commissioner's office, consumer assistance division.

Practicing preventive medicine is the best way to cut health-care costs. The second way is to form an active partnership with a "good" primary-care physician.

Find a good doctor

Of course, a good primary-care doctor plays an important part in your overall health plan, whether you join an HMO or carry other health insurance. If you're not satisfied with the general practitioner you already have, you might try getting names from a nearby medical school or your major hospitals (nursing supervisors often know who the real pros are). Doctors who understand gerontology and geriatrics (the dynamics of aging and the physiology of the older human being) are a good bet. Many medical schools give special courses to train doctors to be aware of the special needs of older patients. For example, when you grow older, the dosage of certain medicines and intensity of certain treatments should be changed, as your body can become much more sensitive to the procedures. Your doctor should be trained in making these adjustments for your individual needs.

Your doctor and Medicare

Some doctors will take what Medicare pays and that's it. Many will not. When a doctor will accept whatever Medicare pays, even though it's below the going rate in your area, that's called accepting "Medicare assignment." Medicare traditionally reimburses below the going rate. That's why a good many doctors these days regularly charge above and beyond what Medicare pays. Whatever your doctor's usual charge is, you should ask him or her to accept Medicare assignment for your bills. Many doctors will accommodate individual patients and take Medicare assignment for them even though they don't do this as a general rule. So be sure to ask. If your doctor refuses to do so, you may want to shop around and find another who will. This may be a difficult task, of course, but it can mean a considerable savings to you on medical bills. (If an HMO participates in Medicare, assignment is automatic.)

A good doctor's office should have staff assistants who can help with Medicare and supplemental insurance claims. In order to get as much as possible out of Medicare your doctor must write up the description of your treatment as fully and completely as possible. Sometimes Medicare refuses to pay its full share because of inadequate information on the claim.

If you have a Medicare claim turned down or whittled down and you feel you are being short-changed, challenge the decision. It's your right to appeal. You can find out where and how from your doctor or from your local Social Security office. Your doctor may be able to offer some additional information that could help you get what's coming to you. Challenge every nonpayment (unless the mistake or misunderstanding is clearly yours). Statistics gathered by the National Senior Law Center show that only 2 percent of the patients who are turned down appeal the decision. But nearly 60 percent of those people who do appeal get the reimbursement they were seeking.

Medicare and supplemental insurance

Because Medicare doesn't pay for everything, you most likely will need supplemental insurance to fill in the gaps.

Medicare reimburses, on the average, only 40 percent of your medical expenses. Basically, for people 65 and above, Medicare provides two types of benefits under two separate parts: Part A and Part B.

Part A provides benefits covering hospital bills and expenses incurred in a skilled nursing facility after a hospital stay. You have to pay certain deductibles, and benefits are limited after 60 days.

Part B is optional. You have to pay a modest monthly fee to get it and it's well worth the money. Charges are deducted from your Social Security checks. With this coverage, 80 percent of what Medicare considers "reasonable" charges for doctor's services is covered. You pay the 20 percent remainder *and* if your doctor charges more than the Medicare "reasonable" rate, you pay the difference also. (This is why it's important to have a doctor who accepts Medicare assignment.)

Under Part A, the skilled nursing care is limited by strict interpretation. It does not cover long-term, "custodial" nursing home care. (Neither do most insurance policies you buy to supplement Medicare.) This is the most worrisome gap in Medicare coverage.

Another major gap is the drop in coverage after 60 days in a hospital. You will have to foot most of the bills unless you have some sort of supplemental insurance coverage or belong to an HMO. But, before you panic, remember that only a tiny fraction of the older patients admitted to hospitals each year stay more than 60 days. For most patients, Medicare covers the bulk of their hospital expenses.

To cover some of the gaps in Medicare coverage, you probably will want to buy supplemental insurance. Supplemental insurance varies in scope and price. Under federal law, Medicare supplemental insurance specifically advertised as such must meet minimum standards, and companies selling the coverage must provide disclosure booklets on just what you're getting and how it fits in with Medicare. Read these carefully. If you have questions, you might discuss them with your doctor or members of his or her office staff.

Buying supplemental insurance can be a confusing and frustrating task. A lot of this confusion is cleared up in *Policy Wise: The Practical Guide to Insurance Decisions for Older Consumers,* an AARP book by consumer protection attorney Nancy H. Chasen. All your options are carefully and clearly spelled out. To order a copy, send a check or money order

payable to AARP Books, 400 South Edward Street, Mount
Prospect, IL 60056. Price: $5.95 + $1.30 shipping and handling. AARP members can obtain the book for $4.35 + $1.30
by writing their membership number on the order.

AARP also has a 23-page booklet called *Information
on Medicare and Health Insurance for Older People.* It explains Medicare terminology and shows how to shop for the
best policy to suit your particular needs. To get a free copy,
write: AARP-Medicare and Health Information, P.O. Box
2400, Long Beach, CA 90801.

Your local Social Security office should have free copies
of two booklets, *Your Medicare Handbook* and *Guide to
Health Insurance for People with Medicare.*

Joseph A. Mintz, an insurance consultant, has a newsletter that covers all sorts of financial subjects for retirees,
including the selection of Medicare supplement insurance.
The newsletter, *Money Management Before and After Retirement,* can be purchased as part of an introductory offer (which
includes a booklet, *Tips and Traps: Combining Medicare with
Your Personal Insurance*). For more information, write: Joseph A. Mintz, NROCA Press, P.O. Box 12066, Dallas, TX
75225.

Armed with this deluge of books and booklets, you
should be able to pick the right policy for your particular
needs. Take the time to sort this supplemental coverage out.
A good deal of money is involved.

Health insurance from age 62 to 65
If you take an early retirement, it's important to obtain health
insurance coverage until Medicare takes over at age 65. Also,
if you're 65 and eligible to receive Medicare but your spouse
is younger, your spouse should obtain health insurance coverage for this interim age period. There are some special "temporary" policies that offer interim coverage for a one-time
premium until permanent health insurance can begin.

Medicaid

If you meet the low-income requirements set by your state, you may be eligible to have Medicaid, a state-administered government health insurance program, take over. Low-income persons of all ages are usually eligible for Medicaid, which assumes nearly all health-care costs. If you think you may be eligible, call your local Social Security office or welfare office.

A final note on Medicare

New legislation calls for a payment plan to be established that will reimburse hospitals for inpatient services at fixed rates according to a diagnostically-related groups classification system instead of the old system of reimbursement for costs. Hospitals will have to absorb any costs above the established fixed rate.

Ready resources

Sourcebook for Older Americans. This book, by attorney Joseph L. Matthews and senior-center director Dorothy Matthews Berman, covers Medicare, Medigap insurance, and Medicaid from top to bottom. The book also covers all phases of Social Security benefits (retirement and disability) and Supplemental Security Income (SSI). For information on how to obtain the book, write: Nolo Press, 950 Parker Street, Berkeley, CA 94710.

Health Self-Appraisal is an elaborate, and relatively inexpensive, computer questionnaire aimed at analyzing your current health situation. You are given your "health age" as opposed to your actual age (it could be up or down depending on the shape you're in). You are also given specific areas for possible self-improvement. For more information, write: Consumer United Group, 2100 M Street, N.W., Washington, DC 20063.

Take Care of Yourself: A Consumer's Guide to Medical Care. Written by Donald M. Vickery, M.D., and James F. Fries, M.D., published by Addison-Wesley, this book shows how to monitor and manage your own health. Some local Blue Cross and Blue Shield offices may have copies.

AARP discount prescriptions by mail. AARP members can save money on medicine, vitamins, sick-room supplies, and health care products through the nonprofit AARP Pharmacy Service. Orders are delivered to homes postpaid. For a listing of locations of AARP pharmacies throughout the country, write AARP Pharmacy Service, Inc., 510 King Street, Suite 426, Alexandria, VA 22314.

Social Security Administration pamphlets. Call or visit your local Social Security office to obtain the following free pamphlets: **SSI for Aged, Disabled, and Blind People; A Brief Explanation of Medicare; Medicare for Federal Employees; Recent Changes in Medicare;** and **A Guide to Supplemental Security Income.**

14
Basic budget
biters

The necessities of daily life, such as food, electricity, and transportation, eat up large chunks of a retirement budget. If you spend some time and effort, you should be able to save some money on essentials that you can then use to pay for special dream items.

Food

Smart shopping is the key to saving money on food without endangering your diet. Here's a quick refresher course on basic smart shopping techniques:

Compare prices at several stores. Generally, large supermarkets have the most competitive prices, and small all-hours convenience stores are the most expensive, but there are exceptions to the rule, so look around.

Buy specials advertised in your local newspaper. Plan your meals around them. Take your list of specials to the store and stick with it.

Stick with house brands and generics. Name brand products carry high advertising costs. House brand products are often the same quality as name brands and are usually cheaper. Generic products have no brand identification and simply list the contents. They're often of a lower quality than house or name brands but offer the same nutritive value and are less expensive. They're worth a try.

Clip coupons. About half the buying public makes use of coupons that offer discounts on retail purchases. If you're a coupon clipper, you can maximize your savings by holding onto coupons until the store runs a sale. For example, if a store is selling a product for 25¢ off its regular price and you have a coupon worth 50¢, you may be able to get the product free or for a very low price.

Join food buying co-ops or clubs. In many areas people have organized food buying clubs or co-ops in order to buy food in large quantities at wholesale prices. Members work together to transport the food, divide it up in small portions, distribute it, and handle bookkeeping. If you're interested in joining or starting a food buying club, write for information to: The Cooperative League of the U.S.A., Suite 1100, 1828 L Street, N.W., Washington, DC 20036.

Grow your own. A home garden can provide you with great produce at a fraction of the store cost, but you've got to be willing to put in some time and effort. If you don't have a plot of your own, you may be able to use ground at little or no cost in a community garden spot in your area. For information, phone the county farm advisor at your local Agriculture Extension Service.

Clothing

If you live in or near a large city, you usually can shop at wholesale or discount clothing stores that have quality brand-name clothing at greatly reduced prices. If you don't live near a big city, you can try ordering clothing through discount mail-order catalogs. Before you order, compare the catalog price with prices at your local stores. Add in postage, sales tax, and other items. *The International Catalogue of Catalogues* (Harper and Row) lists catalogs of all types that you can send for. *Directory of Shop-by Mail Bargain Sources* (Pilot Books) gives hundreds of names and addresses of discounters on all kinds of merchandise.

You might try the resale shops that have become fashionable. These stores accept high-quality, barely used clothing items on consignment and resell them at a fraction of their original cost. Check the phone book Yellow Pages for listings under "Used Clothing."

Utilities
Energy costs can be cut in many different ways, such as closing off unused rooms to conserve heat and/or air conditioning and having your water heater adjusted to a lower temperature. Call your local utility company and ask to have an energy audit made of your home. Utilities are now required to provide customers, on request, a survey of their homes to reveal ways to cut costs—for less than a $15 charge.

Repairs and services
Do-it-yourself skills such as cutting your own hair or reupholstering furniture can help you cut costs in a big way. You might take some courses at your local adult education facility to learn specialized skills such as auto tune-up.

Small-scale, nonprofit community barter groups can offer good opportunities to trade your skills for someone else's. You might trade your home-grown veggies for someone's skills in keeping a car in good running condition. For information on nonprofit barter groups, write to the Barter Project, the National Center for Citizen Involvement, P.O. Box 4179, Boulder, CO 80306.

Transportation
Moving down the demand side of your balance sheet, you come to transportation—getting yourself from here to there the fastest, safest, least expensive way. Because it is a vital part of our lives, we tend to spend a lot of money on transportation. Basically, major transportation costs boil down to an automobile, public transportation, and—for some people—the airlines.

Automobiles

For people who own them, automobiles can be the next most expensive item on their budget list after the purchase and maintenance of a home. A late model car can cost as much as 40 cents a mile to own and maintain. If you drive the average 10,000 miles a year, that's four thousand bucks in depreciation costs, fuel, maintenance, repairs, and insurance.

Obviously, there are great possibilities for savings here. First off, you've got to ask yourself if you really need a car and, if so, must you have access to it on a continuous basis? Think of yourself as a small company with a transportation budget. Is there another way to get wheels without actually owning them?

Renting a car What about renting a car on weekends or for several weeks at a time when you need one? Then, in between rentals, maybe the local bus or rail system could suffice. Or, you might be able to call a cab for certain trips.

If there is no public transportation in your area, or if it is in bad shape and taxis are not available, using a car is a necessity. Find out from car rental agencies in your area what kind of a deal you can get. For example, most companies have special weekend rates because their cars are used primarily for business—Monday through Friday. Some even have overnight specials where you pick up your car after 5 P.M. and bring it back before 9 A.M. the next day.

Use the phone book Yellow Pages (agencies are listed under "Automobile—Renting & Leasing"). Usually, the big names such as Hertz, Avis, and National will quote higher prices—but not always. (AARP members receive discounts of 15 percent off unlimited mileage rates from Hertz and Avis, and 10 percent off from National.) Others such as Dollar, Budget, and Thrifty should have better prices. Then there are the little ones you find at auto dealerships and gas stations. These local companies can sometimes provide excellent trans-

portation at the lowest possible rates. Some will even deliver
the car and pick it up for a modest fee.

By allowing someone else to own the car, you can cut
out a series of heavy ownership costs: depreciation (the drop
in value of your car as it gets older), financing costs, maintenance and repairs, and insurance. With most rental cars, you
are automatically covered for primary insurance. They also
offer a special, daily package for $5 or so to pay for damages
up to the large deductible limit ($500 or more) on the primary
insurance. This daily package is expensive insurance and is
not worth it unless you'll be driving in a difficult area and
want peace of mind.

Obviously, putting together a transportation program
involving periodic car rentals and the use of public transportation and taxis is not for everyone. But, before you shell out
a lot of money for a down payment on a new car and sign
up for expensive financing, think about being a nonowner.
Check it out. Determine just how much you'll be paying
as an owner vs. renting. American Automobile Association
(AAA) offices around the country often have pamphlets that
tell you how to add up the true cost of owning a car. The
Hertz Company also has material on the high cost of ownership.

By not owning a car, you could cut anywhere from
$2,000 to $3,000 off your yearly transportation costs. If you
go the car rental route (plus taxis), you may end up spending
$1,000 to $1,500 a year—but that's still a lot less than owning.
With good public transportation and only occasional car rentals, you could get by for less than $500 a year.

On the subject of public transportation: There may
come a time when you can't drive or don't want to. Then
what? This is why it's so important to line up good transportation services before you decide on buying or renting a home
in a new area. More and more major metropolitan areas
now have subways or excellent bus systems. Some even have

minibuses that feed neighborhood traffic into the main lines.

If you pick a place that's within walking distance of a major shopping and business area (with doctors' offices, clinics, and the like), your feet can handle the bulk of your transportation needs—and keep you in good health. Senior centers, religious organizations, and others occasionally have transportation services for elderly constituents.

Buying a car If you must buy a car, how about a used one? You can buy used cars from Avis, Hertz, and others at considerable discount. You get a near-new car with all the trimmings for much less than it would cost to buy a new one. And you get a warranty. New car dealers often have good buys on cars their customers have turned in—cars they know because they've maintained them.

If you continue to want a new car every three or four years, and there are a lot of retired persons who do, long-term financing (up to 48 months) is a good deal if you need some tax shelter. The interest on the loan is tax deductible (if you're eligible for itemizing).

When you're in the market for a new car, you might want to take a look at the *Car Safety Book,* published and updated each model year by Dr. Leon Robertson, a Yale scientist who has specialized in automobile crash statistics. The book lists most makes and models with an adjacent safety rating based on past accident statistics. On the same line for each make and model, you get the gasoline mileage rating (EPA) and the estimated price. For more information, write: Nanlee Research, 2 Montgomery Parkway, Branford, CT 06405.

Another good consumer reference is *The Car Book: An Indispensable Guide to the Safest Most Economical New Cars,* by Jack Gillis, published and updated each year. Write: The Center for Auto Safety, 1223 Dupont Circle Building, Washington, DC 20036.

When you buy a new car, pretend you're a purchasing agent for a small company. Select the car you want, with the equipment you want (*Consumer Reports* magazine should be of help). Then, ask each dealer who sells the same make and model for the lowest price—a net, driveaway figure.

If possible, don't trade your car in. As a rule, you can get 50 percent more for your old car if you sell it yourself. A gas station or repair shop might fix up your car (nice and shiny) and sell it for you for a commission.

Car insurance You can save money by taking the biggest collision and comprehensive (fire and theft) deductibles you can afford. Many people still have $100 deductible for collision coverage. By doubling this to $200 you can save considerable cash. A good insurance principle is this: Pay for the small stuff yourself and let them cover you for the big items.

Buy liability coverage commensurate with the amount of assets (home, stocks, savings) you might risk in a lawsuit. You can get $300,000 to $500,000 liability coverage for only a few dollars more than for much lower amounts.

Airlines
After your car, travel by air may be next on your list of transportation budget biters. You may be traveling to see children, grandchildren, and others. If so, you should know how to use the airlines. Try to buy your air transportation the way companies do: Use a travel agent.

Travel agents A good travel agent can save lots of time and money. And, in most instances, you don't pay a cent for this extra service. The airlines already have the agents' commissions written into the price of the ticket. So why not take advantage of the service?

How do you find a good agent? The same way you find any other worthwhile professional. Find out if travel-conscious professionals you know (banker, doctor, broker, accountant, lawyer) can recommend a time-tested travel agent. Get names of individuals who have worked well, not just company names.

Once you get a good agent to work with, you're usually set. But, as with any other professional, you need to monitor your agent's performance from time to time to make sure he or she is doing the best possible job for you. Don't just rely totally on the agent. Do some checking yourself.

Your agent should have access to one or two of the airline computer networks. With a computer, the agent can quickly scan flights going to your destination and pick up the best price. You'd have to spend hours doing this kind of search by telephone, and you still might miss the best price. (However, the computer isn't foolproof—all prices are not always fed into the computer, especially those of the smaller airlines.)

With the airlines you have to be careful. The "senior" fare may cost more than other special fares and the "super savers." Example: Regular tourist fare, round trip, from Washington, D.C., to Boston at one time was $189. The "senior" fare was $128. Then came the "super saver" at $111 and, finally, a special "V" fare offered by one airline at $78. A spread of $110.

If you need hotel reservations, a travel agent can line up those too. You could, for example, get a nice lower priced hotel that suits your needs for a third less than the hotel you might have chosen. (AARP members receive 10 percent discounts at various hotels and motels nationwide.)

Airline insurance So far as airline travel insurance (sold at airports and through magazines) is concerned, the kind that covers your life and limbs is usually a waste of money. Presumably, you already have adequate insurance at a much cheaper annual rate per $1,000. If buying this type of insurance gives you peace of mind to allay a fear of flying, then buy it as "therapy." (If you have an American Express card, you get a big chunk of free life and limb insurance every time you use your card for airline travel. It's part of the annual membership dues.)

In general, you should not put articles of any great value in baggage that is being checked. If, per chance, you do include expensive items (such as new dresses, suits, or furs), you might need extra "valuation" coverage from the airline. Otherwise, their payoff liability will be limited. Ask the ticket agent about it.

Ready resources

Cut Your Grocery Bills in Half! Supermarket Survival (Acropolis Books). This book by Barbara Salsbury with Cheri Loveless gives tips that may help you accomplish what the title promises.

The Supermarket Handbook: Access to Whole Foods (New American Library), by Nikki and David Goldbeck, is a shopper's guide to choosing the best foods from those you might find in your local store. It names names, national brands, ingredients, additives, nutritional values, and costs.

Diet for a Small Planet (Ballantine Books), by Frances Moore Lappe, is a classic on healthy eating at low cost.

At Home with Energy and **On the Road with Energy,** 19-page AARP booklets, include checklists for saving energy and cutting energy costs. Write: AARP, 1909 K Street, N.W., Washington, DC 20049.

Policy Wise: The Practical Guide to Insurance Decisions for Older Consumers, an AARP Book by Nancy Chasen, provides checklists for evaluating automobile insurance policies. See Chapter 13 for how to order.

15
Fun and games

Your mortgage, rent, utility bills, repairs, and various types of insurance are heavy hitters on your budget. You've got to pay these bills—no matter what. But there are other items—sometimes equally as important—that are "discretionary." You can take them—or leave them.

Vacation travel

Travel for the fun of it is, perhaps, the leader in this field. The dream of many retired persons is to travel more—to see things they missed when they were working so hard.

But, as you already know, a travel budget can burn up fast. Airlines, hotels, rental cars, and meals away from home gobble up your surplus income. With a little research and creativity, however, you might be able to do better with your travel dollar. Once you've turned 65, airlines, Amtrak, and bus lines offer discounts of 10 percent on up to 33 percent. (Trailways Bus gives AARP members a 12 percent discount.)

As we said in the last chapter, a good travel agent can save you money on airline fares and hotels and other travel fares and fees. Give the travel agent plenty of time before your trip to lock up the biggest discounts before they're sold out.

Travel off-season, if possible. Florida is fine in the summer, and the prices are less than half of what you'd pay in January, February, and March. Food is cheaper and there aren't any lines in the supermarkets. London in the fall and

winter has much better prices than in the summer. You can
see plays, stay at a small but respectable hotel, and visit
the pubs for one-third to one-half of what it would cost in
season. Air fares are much better too.

Have the travel agent pinpoint countries that have de-
valued their currency against the dollar. Mexico, for a while,
was a great bargain. Probably still is. So were Portugal and
Canada.

Some countries give special bonus fares to seniors who
ride their railroads and use their rental cars. Check this out
ahead of time with the agent. You can sometimes get lodging
discounts in this country and abroad. A Golden Age Passport
will give you a 50 percent discount off national park camping
fees. Check out *The Discount Guide for Travelers over 55,*
written by Caroline and Walter Weintz, published by E. P.
Dutton.

Cruises

If you travel off-season with a cruise ship, you can get a
hefty discount. If you travel three or four in a cabin, you
can get a lower rate for the extra passengers. In some cases,
one of the four goes free. If you can drive to the departure
port and accept a standby reservation for one of three dates,
you may qualify for a lower fare.

There's lots of competition in the cruise business these
days. Let them bid for your bucks. Good reading on the
subject: *Answers to the Most-Asked Questions About Cruises,*
Cruise Lines International Association, Pier 35, Suite 200,
San Francisco, CA 94133.

Time sharing

For people who are content with visiting the same vacation
spot year after year, time sharing might do the trick. In effect,
you plunk down considerable cash to buy guaranteed yearly
reservations for a certain period at some mountain or beach

resort. In some cases you may get a tax break on your investment. In other cases you won't. This is a somewhat controver-
sial vacation idea. Some people do very well with it. Others
feel they've been overcharged for what they get. The main
"complaint" is that you're tied to one spot for a "lifetime."
There have also been incidents of fraud and bankruptcy. You
should know whom you're dealing with. Some booklets on
the subject: *Ten Time Share Tips,* Federal Trade Commission,
Office of Consumer Information, Washington, DC 20580. *Resort Time Sharing,* American Land Development Association,
1000 16th Street, N.W., Washington, DC 20008.

Home swapping

Then, there's the whole business of exchanging homes with
someone abroad or here in this country. You sign up for
membership in an association and your home is listed. You
also get a listing of other member's homes. You swap homes
(and cars, too, if you want) according to prearranged plans.
Lots of money can be saved if you research this field with
care. For more information, write: Vacation Exchange Club,
350 Broadway, New York, NY 10013. Or, write: Inquiline,
Inc., 35 Adams Street, Bedford Hills, NY 10507. The former
specializes in home swaps in England, Israel, and Hawaii.
The latter has European homes available.

Campus vacations

To combine a vacation with a learning experience, you might
want to investigate a college or university campus vacation.
Many major universities offer bargain rates for vacations on
campus. You get a good dormitory room, food, stimulating
classes with top-name professors, and side trips to nearby
cities and scenic spots. But you have to write in early. They
fill up their reservation books in a hurry.

Around 600 universities and colleges, in every state
and abroad, are involved in a national informal study program
sponsored by Elderhostel, a nonprofit corporation. If you're

age 60 or older you can enjoy a week's noncredit study with room, meals, and entertainment. Prices are unbelievably low. To get on an Elderhostel catalog mailing list, print your name and address on a postcard and mail to: Elderhostel, 100 Boylston Street, Boston, MA 02116.

A good book on the subject: *Learning Vacations,* by Gerson G. Eisenberg, published by Acropolis Books.

Nomadic living
Thousands of retirees follow the sun north and south, east and west, every year. They travel and live in trailers, motor homes, even mobile homes. It's a nomadic existence, but they seem to thrive on it. They love the camaraderie of trailer parks and campgrounds, they love the open road and, of course, they love the sunshine they're always following.

If you think you have this sort of wanderlust, you should know about the Woodall Publishing company. It's a clearinghouse for all sorts of information on mobile homes, trailers, campers, parks, campgrounds and the like. You get descriptions of camp sites and parks, ratings and prices. The company publishes *Woodall's Campground Directory* and *Woodall's Retirement and Resort Community Guide.* Write: Woodall Publishing Company, 500 Hyacinth Place, Highland Park, IL 60035.

Education
Like vacation travel, the field of continuing education is discretionary so far as your budget is concerned. You don't have to spend money on courses. You can get by without them. But you might miss the experience of a lifetime.

According to Dr. Robert N. Butler, former head of the National Institute on Aging and now gerontology chief at Mt. Sinai School of Medicine in New York, you should invest in your brain as you grow older. Says Butler: "Stretch your head. . . . Keep your memory and your mind active." Otherwise, says Butler, "your mind might start to unplug."

Check out your local community college offerings. Chances are you can get low-cost classes or even free studies if you're over 60 or 65. You'll have hundreds of different courses to choose from. You can take standard literature and English courses, a language, or something more applied such as a course on investment strategies. Some community colleges are doing a booming business with students in their sixties, seventies, and eighties.

Your community college can become a meeting place where you make new friends and keep in touch with what's going on in your field of interest. You might even become a "professor." Many seniors do. All you need is a subject you're an expert on and at least ten to twenty students. The pay is just fair, but the "psychic income" is great. You impart the knowledge and experience of years to others who are eager to soak it up. For more information on possible community college programs in your area, write: American Association of Community Colleges, One Dupont Circle, Suite 410, Washington, DC 20036.

In every state there are colleges and universities that also offer tuition breaks to older persons. At many schools anyone over age 60 or 65 can take almost any course in a continuing education curriculum at no charge so long as there's room on the roster. Other schools offer a series of noncredit courses for seniors for less than the cost of a light lunch. For a listing of colleges in your state that offer free or reduced tuition, write: The Institute of Lifetime Learning, AARP, 1909 K St., N.W., Washington, DC 20049.

The National Council on Aging (NCOA) sponsors a Senior Center Humanities Program that has been most successful. Some 70,000 retired people have taken the humanities courses, which are offered free through 1,400 senior centers in 49 states.

NCOA furnishes the study-unit anthologies on such subjects as literature, philosophy, history, anthropology, folklore, and the visual arts. Students have written poems, essays, and short stories that have been published. Some have written histories of their towns or neighborhoods and have appeared on TV as local "experts." Says one Maryland graduate in her seventies: "These courses helped me to realize more than ever that age is no deterrent to the things you like to do. . . . As long as one lives there is always something new to learn." For more information about courses in your area or about the possibility of having your organization start up some courses, write: The National Council on Aging, 600 Maryland Avenue, S.W., Washington, DC 20024.

An informative free booklet, *Learning Opportunities for Older Persons,* is available by writing: Institute of Lifetime Learning, AARP, 1909 K Street, N.W., Washington, DC 20049. The booklet outlines a number of options for learning, including noncredit and degree courses, college credit for life experience, and home study and correspondence courses.

The Institute also produces a series of minicourses on various subjects—booklets designed for use in small discussion groups or by individuals. To obtain free single copies or multiples, write to the Institute for an order form.

If you prefer to study at home at your own pace, you can enroll in correspondence and home study programs offered by colleges, universities, and private organizations. You can earn high school or college credits or take noncredit courses for your own enjoyment.

The Guide to Independent Study Through Correspondence is available for $5.95 plus $1.25 postage and handling from the National University Continuing Education Association, Book Order Department, P.O. Box 2123, Princeton, NJ 08540. This publication lists credit and noncredit correspondence courses at junior high, high school, and college levels offered by accredited institutions of higher education belonging to the association.

The free *Directory of Accredited Home Study Schools*

is available from The National Home Study Council, repre-
senting 109 private correspondence schools that offer courses
of mainly a technical/vocational nature. Write: NHSC, 1601
18th Street, N.W., Washington, DC 20009.

Gastro-economics

We've already covered the subject of basic food costs along
with such regular budget biter items as clothing and utilities.
But the basics are not what we're concerned with here. Food
is a necessity. But it can also be a pleasurable experience—
a form of entertainment.

You'll want to eat out from time to time or, perhaps,
have others over to your place. Having round-robin gourmet
sessions can provide a lot of entertainment and good food
at bargain prices. One group has an eat-in at a member's
house once a month. Each time the theme involves a country's
typical food or regional dishes. One night you're in Japan.
Another night you're in Mexico. You get food at one-third
the cost of eating out plus lots of companionship.

If you eat out at a good restaurant, you can save money
and really get enough to eat by selecting two appetizers instead
of a full-course dinner. Try soup and scallops. Or, clams
Casino and a Caesar salad. The bill won't be overloaded
and neither will your stomach.

In many areas, top-line restaurants have pre-theater,
prix-fixe dinners at almost half the going price. In general,
if you're willing to eat a little earlier, you'll be eligible for
a good discount. Same goes for smaller portions. Check your
phone book Yellow Pages, under "Restaurants," to see who's
offering the early-bird or pre-theater discounts. Also, in many
cities, you can purchase coupon books that give you a year's
worth of "buy one meal, get one free" coupons for participating restaurants. Inquire about possible coupon book offers
at your local Chamber of Commerce.

Ready resources

House exchanges
Vacation Exchange Club, 350 Broadway, New York, NY 10013.

Travel on land and water
BritRail Pass, 630 Third Avenue, New York, NY 10017.

Eurail Pass, c/o French National Railroad, 610 Fifth Avenue, New York, NY 10111.

Floating through Europe, 271 Madison Avenue, New York, NY 10016. Free brochure on water travel in Britain and Europe.

Grand Circle Travel, Inc., 555 Madison Avenue, New York, NY 10022. Free information on tours and cruises.

AARP Travel Service, administered by Olson-Travelworld, Ltd., 5855 Green Valley Circle, Culver City, CA 90230. Free AARP Travel Planner with information on AARP tours, regional vacations, and leisure holidays in the U.S.A. and many different countries. Write: AARP Travel Service, P.O. Box 92337, Los Angeles CA 90009.

Pearl's Freighter Tips, Suite 306R, 175 Great Neck Road, Great Neck, NY 11021. Free information on freighter travel.

Vacations and camping outdoors
National Park Service, U.S. Department of the Interior, 18th and C Streets, N.W., Washington, DC 20240. Information on Golden age (62+) and Golden Eagle (under 62) passes plus information about national parks.

Farm and Ranch Vacations, Inc., 36 E. 57th Street, New York, NY 10022.

Medical help overseas
Intermedic, Inc., 777 Third Avenue, New York, NY 10017.

International Association for Medical Assistance to Travelers, 350 Fifth Avenue, New York, NY 10001.

Travel guides
Mobil travel guides. Published annually by Rand McNally & Co.

Fodor, Fielding, Frommer, or Michelin guides for travel abroad only.

Educational opportunities information
The National Registration Center for Study Abroad (NRCSA), 823 N. 2nd Street, Milwaukee, WI 53203. Information on over 3,000 study programs sponsored by over 240 foreign sponsors.

College Level Examination Program, Educational Testing Service, P.O. Box 592, Princeton, NJ 08540. Information about CLEP, a program for earning college credits by examination.

Council for the Advancement of Experiential Learning, 300 Lakefront North, Columbia, MD 21044. Information on learning institutions giving credits for job or life experiences.

National Center for Educational Brokering, 325 9th Street, San Francisco, CA 94103. Information on how brokers can counsel adults on choosing educational programs, especially for job training.

16
Credit and debt

Borrowing money is a way of life in this country. Some might say it is *the* way of life. Many of us borrow to finance our homes, cars, and other major purchases. Many of us borrow through credit cards. As a matter of fact, the majority of credit card holders across the land borrow all the time through revolving credit. They just keep on paying the high interest rates (18 to 22 percent annually) month after month, year after year.

When a person retires, according to the classic image, a happy smile denotes a state of well-being because the mortgage and all other long-term debts have been paid off. No more loans. It's nice to know that you don't owe anybody anything. But, beyond that feeling of freedom, being completely out of debt may not be indicative of sound financial planning. Of course, being up to your ears in debt, with a dozen credit card companies clamoring for your hide, is no way to live either.

Creative credit
The trick is to use OPM (Other Peoples' Money) when it serves your financial needs. As long as you can easily make the monthly payments on your retirement income, it may be to your advantage to have a new loan on your home and financing for your car, especially if you're paying high income taxes. You get a hefty deduction for all that interest you're paying out.

If your mortgage goes for 13 percent and you're in the 33 percent tax bracket (in the low $20,000 a year range), you knock off one-third of the interest rate to calculate your true loan cost (after taxes). In this case it would be slightly less than 9 percent. As we mentioned earlier, you can figure your tax bracket this way: Divide your gross federal and state tax (before credits) by your taxable income. For example, if the combined gross tax is $6,000 and taxable income is $20,000, the tax bracket is 30 percent.

We've already talked about home mortgages in previous chapters. But you might want a tax adviser to review your situation to make sure you're making the proper use of mortgage debt as a way to reduce the tax bite.

You might be resisting this kind of talk about "creative credit" because you're the kind of person who just doesn't want to be in debt. You feel uneasy with it and want to stay free and clear. Fine. You're better off working on a cash basis. It's important for your mental health to stay debt free.

The rest of us are usually not so put off by the word *credit*. It brings us nice things and organizes our spending. It's kind of like forced savings. You go into hock for a car and then put aside so much money every month for the payments. A cash-and-carry person would spend many months, maybe many years, saving for a new car. Meanwhile, he or she might be driving a heap that costs more than it's worth to repair.

Personal loans

If you've got a good credit rating and are in good standing at your bank, you probably can get a personal loan with no collateral required. This is an unsecured loan. They're lending you the money on your good name. If they want access to your savings account, your car, your furniture, what-

ever, then you have a secured loan. If you don't pay, they
take the money out of your savings, take your car back, or
take your furniture. You can pledge stocks, bonds, savings
certificates—even your home (but don't do this last one without the advice of an attorney).

Revolving credit cards

Borrowing money with a revolving credit card can be a convenience or a conflagration. If you go into debt on occasion
to pick up a bargain purchase or have emergency repairs
done on your car, that's a wise use of borrowing power.
But, if you're constantly paying less than the full amount
owed, you're burning up your budget with high interest
charges.

Never get hooked on paying the "Minimum Due." Pay
off as much as you can as soon as you can. Get out of revolving
credit as soon as possible. If every bank card holder paid
the total due each month, it would bust the business. They'd
go broke. As it stands, they're making money because the
vast majority of cardholders pay less than the total due—
month after month.

Pay-in-full credit cards

There are certain types of credit cards that are, in a sense,
"debt proof." They won't let you borrow. You pay what's
due, when it's due. If you don't, they send you increasingly
nasty notes and eventually cut you off.

American Express, Diners Club, and Carte Blanche
are types of cards that do not allow revolving credit. You
can, occasionally, charge a package tour or something like
it and pay with installments. But your regular purchases must
be paid up each month. These cards, called T & E (for travel
and entertainment), require an annual membership fee.

In a sense, when you use a card that doesn't permit

revolving credit, you're getting somebody else's money for a period of time without paying for the privilege. You buy a dinner with the card. But you don't pay for it until a month, sometimes longer, has passed. You may be billed 30 days after your purchase and, on top of that, you've got another 25 days or so to pay your bill. This is called a "float" in financial circles. You get the use of goods and services for short periods without having to pay for them. Over the years, this can add up to quite a saving. You can keep your money longer in acounts where it can gather more interest. (If you pay the full balance on revolving credit cards, you get the same "float".)

There's another factor. People who sell the goods and services that are purchased with credit cards have already adjusted their general prices upward to offset the cost of the credit. If you don't make full use of this float convenience, you're paying for the credit privilege without using it.

Debit cards

There's another kind of card that often looks like a credit card but isn't. It's a debit card. MasterCard and Visa have debit cards as well as credit cards, and so do several bank holding companies and money market funds. With a debit card your purchases are tied directly to a checking or savings account. The card is like a plastic check that you can use to buy things in areas where no one would want to take your personal check. Every time you use your debit card, you should deduct the amount paid from your last balance— just like keeping your checkbook current. The disadvantage with debit cards is that you lose your "float." Money is trans-ferred the same day you make your purchase.

As a rule, you don't pay an annual fee for a debit card. You do have to pay for Visa and MasterCard credit cards (from $15 to $20 a year). Having a debit card or a T & E charge card is a good way to avoid the revolving credit trap. Some oil companies also have pay-in-full charge cards.

Credit laws and regulations

A number of federal laws govern the issuing and operation of credit cards. The *Equal Credit Opportunities Act* protects you against credit discrimination. You can't be denied credit because of your age or sex and—most important—you can't be forced to take out credit life insurance because of your age.

Credit life insurance pays off if you die owing money. Although it is often heavily promoted by salespeople, credit life insurance in general is not a good buy. If you have enough insurance, don't pay extra for this debt-related coverage.

There is an interesting exception to the rule. If you need life insurance to protect your spouse or other dependent, and if you can't get any coverage because of your age or your health, then credit life insurance is not a bad bet.

We know of an aging Texan who has a heart condition and cannot get insurance. He has credit life policies on his home loan, auto loan, boat loan—anything he can get his hands on. Because credit life issuers usually don't require a medical exam, this fellow's only chance for coverage is through his debts. If he dies, his home will be paid up. So will his car and boat. His widow can turn these assets into cash if she wishes.

The *Fair Credit Billing Act* protects you against creditors who make mistakes and don't correct them. If you receive a bill you think is incorrect, the first thing to do is pay the portion that is correct. This way, you show the creditor you're operating in good faith. Then, you write to the creditor explaining why you think there's an error. Your complaint must be in writing to be legally valid. Mail this letter as soon as you can but no later than 60 days after you get your bill. The law makes it mandatory for the creditor to review the error and correct it quickly.

Another provision of the law covers credit card purchases of merchandise that turns out to be defective or not what the seller promised. Although the Fair Credit Billing

Act requires the purchase to be within a 100-mile radius of your home and in excess of $50, you can use the protection for items ordered by mail. The Federal Trade Commission (the government agency monitoring the law) says a mail-order transaction usually is considered to take place in your home because that's where the order blank is filled out or phoned in through a toll-free number. If something goes wrong, you just pay for the portion that's correct. Don't send in the money related to the erroneous item. Always explain your action with a prompt letter (and keep a copy).

According to the FTC rules and regulations, creditors are limited in their efforts to dun you for debts. They must not call up at odd hours. They must not call repeatedly as a form of harrassment. They can't use threats.

If you think a creditor is picking on you, get in touch with your local consumer protection agency (state, county, or city). Ask for help. As a rule, a protection agency attorney or paralegal will tell the creditor to cool it. If you can't find an agency nearby, write: The Federal Trade Commission, Bureau of Consumer Protection, Washington, DC 20580. Ask for booklets and pamphlets that explain your rights as a debtor.

Under the *Fair Credit Reporting Act,* you have the right to see your record at the credit bureau that covers your area. If you have been denied credit, you can ask for a review of your record to see what was wrong. There will be no charge. If you just want to see what your credit record looks like, there may be a small charge (about $5).

Basically, a credit bureau doesn't deny credit. The merchant or credit card company does the denying based on information about you in the bureau's file. If you pay your bills late or have bad debts outstanding, it's noted in your file. Sometimes, though, the information in the file is wrong. If so, you can have it expunged. It's your right.

Help for debt problems

If you get into trouble with your debts, don't duck the issue. Get help. You may have had a pile of unreimbursed medical bills. You may have lost a part-time job or had some other calamity descend on you. If so, let your creditors know about it. Most will be sympathetic, especially if you've been a faithful customer. They may stretch out your debt or hold repayment demands until you get on your feet.

But there are a few creditors who want their money *now*. Anyone who doesn't pay on time, in their minds, is an automatic deadbeat. If you have serious problems with a creditor like this or if you've gotten into debt too deep, you should seek counseling.

Debt counseling

The Consumer Credit Counseling Service offers assistance to people who are having difficulties with debts. They can get in touch with your creditors and arrange a stretched- . out debt payment schedule. You pay them a weekly or monthly lump sum and they disburse it to the creditors. In most states, there's a very modest charge for this service. For information about a Consumer Credit Counseling Service near you, write: National Foundation for Consumer Credit, 8701 Georgia Avenue, Suite 601, Silver Springs, MD 20910 (301-589-5600). Your bank manager, credit union loan officer, store credit manager, or such government agencies as your local consumer protection office or Area Agency on Aging also should be able to guide you toward proper debt counseling services.

Counseling is not "debt consolidation." Debt consolidation is an arrangement offered by a loan company. The loan company lends you a lump sum which you use to pay off your individual debts. Then, you pay off the loan company over a longer period of time with a higher interest rate to

contend with. *Don't* get into a costly debt consolidation contract (actually illegal in some states) if you can avoid it. *Do*
get legitimate debt counseling and payment services.

Protection of the court

If you really get into debt and can't seem to find a way
out, you may need protection of the court. Federal Bankruptcy Courts have Chapter 13 sections, which allow you
to pay off your debts over a two- to three-year period under
the protection of the court. You may have some of your
debts reduced, the payments may be stretched out, and all
the late charges and interest may be erased.

Although this procedure is handled through the bankruptcy court, it's not "going bankrupt." You are paying off
your debts, not wiping them out. This option is open to people
who have jobs, part time or full time, and/or other steady
income. You'll need an attorney, and the court usually provides you a list of lawyers in the area who specialize in bankruptcy law.

Remember, these tips on debt counseling and bankruptcy court are for your "emergency drawer." You probably
won't need them. Meanwhile, it's nice to know your rights
and options—just in case.

17
Paying less tax

You should take every measure possible to reduce your income tax bills. The law says you only have to pay what you owe. Unfortunately, all too many older taxpayers pay *more* than they owe because they're unaware of special deductions, credits, and exemptions. Basically there are two concepts to explore for tax-saving possibilities: (1) tax planning, and (2) tax return preparation.

Tax planning
This usually involves sitting down with a tax expert (accountant, lawyer, or financial planner) to study your personal financial situation. The tax planner will need your recent returns and all your personal balance sheet information (outlined in Chapter 3). What debts do you have? What income? What assets? That sort of thing. Most tax planners will give you a checklist of information they'll need to do the job right.

How much does all this cost? A good tax planner will charge $45 to $95 an hour, depending on where you live and what kind of a planner you get. Lawyers usually charge more than accountants. Financial planners usually charge less than accountants or don't charge at all if you buy investments through their companies.

Do it-yourself planning
If you want to do the job yourself to save on the fees, you'll need to do some homework. You'll have to know how to

draw up your personal financial statement, and you'll have to know where to look for the major tax savings.

Fortunately, libraries and bookstores are loaded with books on how to save money on your taxes. Look them over to see which seem to fit your particular needs. Some recommendations: *Perfectly Legal—300 Methods for Paying Less Taxes* (Wiley), by Barry Steiner, CPA, and David Kennedy, MBA, JD, works through a question-and-answer format, covering an extensive list of tax situations. *How to Save 50 Percent or More on Your Income Tax* (Macmillan), by California tax attorney B. Ray Anderson, is a tax-planning guide aimed at people who have incomes from $14,000 to $49,000.

Although these books can give you a crash course in tax planning, they can't do the job of a professional tax planner. If you're paying a fairly hefty income tax, every penny you pay a tax planner is usually worth it. For a relatively modest fee, you could save thousands of dollars in reduced taxes.

Finding a planner

How do you find a good tax planner? The same way you find other key professionals. By word-of-mouth references. Your doctor, dentist, and lawyer often know the names of good tax people. After all, they usually have high incomes, and paying less taxes should be vital interest to them.

Tax-saving areas

Some tax-saving areas that could be explored in tax planning sessions are the following:

Your home If you're buying or selling a home, a tax planner can discuss ways of cutting your tax bill. The $125,000 once-in-a-lifetime exemption from taxes on capital gains you might make on a home sale should be a key item. The planner should tell you whether it's better to take the exemption now or—if you're not realizing much profit—to hold it in reserve for the future. A planner should also warn you about marrying someone who has already taken this once-in-a-lifetime tax break. It could take away your exemption. Selling your home *before* the marriage could do the trick. You should also be given a detailed checklist on possible home improvements and repair costs that could reduce any tax you might have to pay on the sale of your home.

If you're doing your own tax planning or want to be better informed when you talk to a professional planner, look over IRS Publication #523, *Tax Information on Selling Your Home*. It includes information on the $125,000 exemption and on deductions you can take for home improvements and other expenses. (Some home improvements that save energy, such as insulation, entitle you to residential energy credits on your tax return.)

Your home business One of the best ways to get a bunch of tax deductions and credits is to start up a little business in your home. It could be a manufacturing business (leather products) or a service (tutoring). You may be able to write off a number of items you would have to pay for anyway. But there are rules and restrictions that may limit how much of a tax break, if any, you can get. A tax planner can give you a checklist of the deductions and credits you can legally take. The planner can also help you set up your books to make future tax preparation easier.

If you're a do-it-yourselfer, or if you want to be better prepared to talk to a tax planner, check out IRS Publication #587, *Business Use of Your Home*.

Rental properties If you own a rental property or rent out a room in your home, or if you plan to become a mini-landlord some day (even if you have a relative as a tenant), a tax planner can show how to make the most of it. One of the most important items for landlords is the depreciation allowance. With commercial property, the value is reduced year by year, according to a calculated depreciation schedule. This can reduce your income tax in big chunks—right away. You also can get valuable deductions for expenses involved in your rental property.

For more information on the subject, read IRS Publication #527, *Rental Property.*

Profits and losses If you sell property (real estate, stocks) that has appreciated or dropped in value, your planner might be able to save you some money. In general, profits on property owned for more than one year qualify for special long-term capital gains treatment. Only 40 percent of long-term capital gains is subject to income tax. Naturally, if you don't sell the property, you only have a paper profit and no tax is due.

If you sell something at a loss *before* a year of ownership runs out, you may qualify for a *full* tax deduction up to $3,000 per year. If the loss is taken after one year of ownership, you can take only half the deduction. Since the rules on capital gains and losses are very complex, a tax planner can give you pin-point advice on when to sell property to qualify for the best tax treatment possible.

Tax-deferred pension plans If you have any kind of pension money that is tax deferred, a planner may be able to help with the timing and distribution schedule to provide the best tax benefits.

Marital status If you're contemplating marriage or divorce, there are important tax ramifications. A planner can point them out. For example: alimony is taxable to the recipient; support for a dependent is not. A widow or widower may also be eligible for special tax treatment. A bereaved spouse may be able to file a joint return, which gives a better break than a single return, for the year in which the partner dies. And special tax treatment is given to the survivor when the home is sold (higher "basis" cost to cut down any taxable profit).

Investment strategy If you're in a tax bracket of 33 percent or better (low $20,000 range), you might benefit from a tax-sheltered investment such as a limited partnership, rental property, or tax-free bonds. A planner can advise you on which of these options is best for you.

These are just some of the areas that are open to money-saving tax planning. There are others. A tax planner will go over a complete questionnaire checklist to make sure he or she has all the information necessary to do your "tax profile." Once you see where you stand, you probably won't need another planning session for a while (until there's a major change in your life).

Tax return preparation

The second area of tax expertise is the actual preparation of your return. Proper preparation requires current knowledge of tax laws, of IRS rulings, and of court cases.

Do-it-yourself preparation

If your return is fairly simple, you may be able to prepare it yourself or do it with free Tax-Aide program help for older persons sponsored by AARP. Call your local IRS office to find out the location of an Aide office in your area. The work is done by trained older volunteers and there is no charge.

The booklet *Your Retirement Income Tax Guide*, free from AARP, P.O. Box 2400, Long Beach, CA 90801, has all the recent tax law changes and a checklist of items of particular interest to retired taxpayers.

It tells you who has to file and who doesn't. But, even

if you think your taxable income is too low for filing, it might be a good idea to do so anyway. This way you're on record. And, if you've worked, you'll want to recover taxes withheld from your wages. The IRS is governed by a statute of limitations (they can order an audit up to three years after you file). But if you don't file and a problem crops up after the three-year period, they can go after you.

Professional preparation

If you're reading this book, chances are you have income other than Social Security (which is tax free up to a certain level of income). Even if you've been doing your tax return yourself, it's not a bad idea to have a professional or an AARP Tax-Aide person take a crack at it once in a while to see if there are money-saving maneuvers you have overlooked. And a good preparer may get in some tax planning time which could save money on future tax returns.

Estimated tax payments

One area of confusion that an expert preparer can clear up is the whole business of filing estimated tax payments on a quarterly basis. If you have income from savings, a pension fund, investments, or whatever that isn't subject to any withholding, you may have to make quarterly tax payments based on your estimated annual income. A tax preparer can tell you just how much your estimated income might be and the payment amount you should mail in to the IRS every three months. Your local IRS office or AARP Tax-Aide Service may also be able to give you guidance on this if you don't want to buy a tax preparer's time.

Finding a tax preparer

You can find a tax preparer through word-of-mouth recommendations (doctor, banker, lawyer, etc.) or by looking under "Tax Return Preparation" in the phone book Yellow Pages.

A good tax preparer should be working in the tax trade all year long, not just at tax time. He or she should have subscriptions to current tax law information services such as Commerce Clearinghouse, Research Institute of America, or Prentice Hall. An accountant who specializes in taxes can be of particular help if you're involved with a home business or rental property. He or she can help with business planning and accounting procedures. (More on accountants in Chapter 19.)

Some overlooked tax deductions

You can get an income adjustment (downward) by subtracting any penalties savings institutions imposed because you withdrew your money before the maturity date.

You can deduct transportation costs for business use of your car or use of your car for certified medical trips (doctor, clinic, dentist, whatever). You can deduct mileage costs for the use of your car as a volunteer (such as church business).

Here's a rundown of other often-overlooked deductions for people who itemize, as compiled by the accounting firm of Deloitte, Haskins and Sells:

Sales tax deductions The sales tax on the following items can be deducted *in addition to* the amount determined by using the optional sales tax tables prepared by the IRS: car, motorcycle, motor home, truck, boat, plane, or materials used to build a new home.

Points charged for mortgages You can deduct in full any points you pay on your mortgage for a new home or addition to the home in the year of payment, regardless of whether they represent a prepayment, so long as the following conditions are met: (1) the points charged must be in line with other similar agreements in your area; (2) the points must be charged for use of money, not services; and (3) the loan must be a conventional loan (not financed through FHA, VA, or any other such method).

Finance charges Any finance charges you pay on installment accounts (credit cards) or on retail or educational institution contracts are tax deductible.

Securities that have become worthless For the tax year in which the securities went under, you may claim a full short-term capital loss even though you still hold the shares.

Uncollectible personal loans You can usually deduct these as short-term capital losses.

Tax return and tax planning fees The money you pay a professional tax preparer and/or planner is deductible. Your cab fares or auto mileage to and from the tax professional's office (plus the parking fee) are also deductible, as are payments for tax books and seminars.

State and local taxes Any state or local income taxes that were paid or withheld from your salary during the previous year are deductible. If additional state or local taxes have been assessed against you because of an audit of a prior year's return, any additional tax, as well as interest, is deductible in the year it is paid. Local property taxes are also deductible, as are the state sales taxes mentioned earlier.

State and local tax breaks
Local property tax laws and policies, by the way, should be carefully checked for money-saving possibilities. A number of states give special breaks to senior taxpayers. For example, New Jersey adds $50 to its property tax rebates. In Illinois,

you get a reduction in the assessed value of your home. In Alaska, there's no property tax on your home. A good booklet, *Your Retirement State Tax Guide,* is available from: AARP, P.O. Box 2400, Long Beach, CA 90801. It covers state income tax breaks for seniors as well as property tax breaks (where they exist).

Deductions for charitable gifts

If you are able to itemize your deductions, you can get all sorts of tax breaks from gifts to charitable or other tax-exempt institutions. For taxpayers who don't itemize, there's a small deduction available.

When you donate property to a charity (furniture, clothing, appliances), you have to list the "fair market value." What would you pay for it or what could you sell it for? An educated guess will do. Write up an inventory of the items, put down an estimated value for each, and get the charity to sign or stamp your list. Or, get any kind of receipt you can and staple it to your inventory. This will nail down your deduction in case you're challenged.

If you have property that has appreciated substantially in value, it's better for donations than actual cash. You get a deduction for the current market value, and you don't have to pay any capital gains tax.

The firm of Deloitte, Haskins and Sells describes several ways of giving property to a charity while continuing to enjoy the property during your lifetime (and your spouse's lifetime):

Future interests in real estate A personal residence, including a vacation home, can be a highly useful vehicle for charitable giving that is free from the restrictions attached to other forms of deferred giving. You can give such a residence to a qualified charity now and yet retain possession of the facility for your lifetime and that of your spouse. You obtain an immediate tax deduction for a portion of the property's value. The charity receives the benefits after the death of the surviving spouse.

Remainder trusts A charitable remainder trust is another vehicle by which a donor of property can receive an immediate income tax deduction (equal to an actuarily computed present value of the property) and retain the income interest in the property transferred to the trust. Also, if the property has appreciated in value, the donor does not have to pay capital gains tax. Of course, your heirs won't get the property when you die.

Ready resources

Your Federal Income Tax, published by the Internal Revenue Service, free of charge. Must reading for anyone who wants to do his or her own tax return or wants to ask intelligent questions during the interview with a professional tax planner or tax preparer. Call your local IRS office for any IRS publications.

IRS Schedules R and RP, Credit for the Elderly. These forms explain how you might get a special tax break if very little, if any, of your retirement income comes from Social Security or any of the other tax-free retirement benefit sources.

18
Estate planning

In the previous chapter we were involved with current taxes on income and property. Now we're going to tackle the future tax problem—the one your beneficiaries may face when you die. For current tax work, you may want to have a tax planner, as we mentioned. For taxes involving the transfer of property at your death, you usually need an estate planner. A lawyer who specializes in estate tax work should do the job, if at all possible.

If your net worth is modest and made up of very few items, your estate plan may simply consist of a will. And you may be able to obtain sufficient legal advice in drawing up your will for little or no cost from your Area Agency on Aging or local Legal Aid Society. You may not need to hire a lawyer.

But if you have a substantial estate, or net worth, or if you have assets in complicated forms, you require the specialized help of an attorney familiar with estate tax planning. The bigger your estate, the more you need the help of an expert.

The estate planning process involves deciding how your property should be currently owned (jointly, separately, in trust, or whatever). It involves drawing up a will or revising an old will. And it involves reviewing the kinds of investments you hold: stocks, bonds, annuities, insurance, real estate, and the like.

Review your will

If you have not reviewed your estate or your will recently—
even if yours is a modest estate—you'd better do so now.
A while back, the federal estate tax laws were changed to
greatly benefit beneficiaries of small- to medium-sized estates.
On estates left to anyone, no federal estate taxes are due
on amounts up to $325,000 in 1984. This will increase yearly
on up to $600,000 in 1987. Unlimited amounts now go tax-
free to surviving spouses, but only if specific wording is used
in a will: "I wish to leave my spouse my entire estate under
the unlimited marital deduction as of August 13, 1981." This
wording must be used instead of the old standard legal wording: "I give my wife/husband an equal amount to the maximum marital deduction." The old phrase *maximum marital
deduction* will be interpreted under the old law—usually half
the estate or $250,000, whichever is more.

If you have moved, married, been widowed or divorced
since you had your will made, or if beneficiaries have died,
been divorced, gotten married, or fallen out of favor, your
will should be changed. You can make minor changes in
your will through codocils that are inserted in the proper
legal language by a lawyer and then initialed by you and
witnessed. But if you have substantial changes to make, you
should have a completely new will drawn up.

Work with a lawyer

If you don't already have a good lawyer, you can select the
right person through the usual search method. Ask other
professionals (banker, doctor, accountant, and the like) for
names. As a rule, a preliminary "get acquainted" visit doesn't
require a fee. Ask about a fee when you arrange this visit.
If you find you don't get along well with the lawyer, try
others. See Chapter 19 for more information on lawyers and
fees.

Organize information

Once you've selected a lawyer, you can save considerable time—and money—by doing some homework before you come in for your first business visit. The lawyer will need to know all about you and your beneficiaries: names, addresses, Social Security numbers, birthdates; your total assets and debts; the way property is held (jointly or individually); life insurance policies—the works. Most attorneys have questionnaires or fact sheets you can fill out at home. This helps with the organization of your financial data.

You can get off to a good start on your own by filling out Worksheet 7 at the end of this chapter. Check off all your important papers, indicate how they are held, and show where they are located.

Consider terms of your will

Once you've gotten all your information lined up, you'll have to consider who gets what in your will. Your family probably comes first. But who will get what and in what proportion? Will there be anything for friends? Anything for some favored charity?

Perhaps you think you can save money by not having a will. You might think all you have to do is to have your property jointly owned—if you're married—and then everything will go automatically to your spouse. It isn't all that easy. Your children may have their inheritance reduced when your spouse dies. A will is more flexible. You can have your estate divided into portions. And putting a will together serves as a psychological or emotional focal point. There's a satisfaction that comes with sorting out all your earthly belongings and arranging for an orderly transfer to the ones you love.

A lawyer will know whether your old will is still valid. When you move from one state to another, you're under a different set of laws. You may have to have your will updated.

A lawyer specializing in estate law will also tell you about "liquidity" and your estate. If your wealth is all tied up in land or other forms of hard-to-sell assets, there may not be enough ready cash to pay off your debts and final expenses. If this is the case, the lawyer might suggest that you convert some of your assets into an easy-access investment such as a jointly owned money market mutual fund or money market savings account.

A lawyer will go into the technicalities of dual deaths. If you and your spouse are in an accident and you die together or one of you lives a few days longer, tax and probate complications could arise. Your estate might be excessively taxed. All sorts of probabilities and chance should be sorted out for a husband and wife team, especially if they plan to travel a lot together. Proper wording of your will and deciding how property should be held can prevent future problems.

Consider trusts

Then there's the whole field of trusts. Trusts involve drawing up a legal agreement to turn over certain assets to the care of someone else (a trustee) to hold and manage for the benefit of a third part (a beneficiary). A trust created during your lifetime is called a living trust. A trust that is established in your will and which becomes operative upon your death is called a testamentary trust. Living trusts can be revocable (you can change or cancel) or irrevocable.

Trusts most often are used to avoid or postpone taxes, to ensure that the trustmaker's wishes are carried out upon death, and to obtain professional management of financial affairs.

One popular type of trust called a "bypass" trust is especially designed to save on estate taxes when the surviving spouse (the beneficiary of the trust) dies.

Trusts are also used to protect beneficiaries from making unwise financial decisions. For example, you might not think that a grandchild would be able to manage the amount of money you're leaving until he or she was older and more settled. You could have a trust written so that the grandchild wouldn't get any income until age 25 or later. Income could be paid out by the trustee if it was felt the grandchild had a real need for the money (education, cultural trip abroad, or starting a new business). Then, at age 30 the grandchild could get control of half the funds. At 35 the remainder could be given over.

As an alternative to trusts, while you're alive you can give up to $10,000 a year ($20,000 for a husband and wife filing a joint tax return) to a child or grandchild or any number of individual recipients without incurring a gift tax. You reduce the amount of your estate, thus reducing possible estate taxes, and you have the joy of giving.

Trusts are not for everyone. But you should have a lawyer explain the pros and cons of particular kinds of trusts relative to your own financial situation. A trustee has to be named to manage the trust. You might want your spouse or some other relative to act as co-trustee with a more financially knowledgeable person.

Evaluate joint ownership

You may have your home, your car, and other property held jointly with your spouse. When you die, this property automatically goes to the survivor outside a will. No taxes. No probate. It seems neat and tidy. But estate planning lawyers say there *are* situations where this kind of ownership is not wise. It might mess up an estate and force a bigger tax payment when the surviving spouse dies. It's rather complicated, and you should put down "joint ownership" on your list of questions for your lawyer. Maybe your jointly owned property is okay. Maybe it isn't.

Name an executor

Another question that should be answered, after some reflection, is: Who will be the executor of your estate? It's a tough job. You should pick someone who has a sense of business or property management and can be trusted to carry out the terms of your will. You can't always find this combination. If not, you might consider having a lawyer be a co-executor with a relative. These professionals, of course, will charge a fee and that has to be considered. Be sure to nominate a contingent executor in case your first choice can't do the job. You should also nominate contingent beneficiaries for your insurance in case the named beneficiary dies.

Check your insurance
At this point, you might review your insurance policies to see if you have enough in there to take care of the immediate cash needs of your spouse or other survivor you named. Perhaps, you have too much insurance. Maybe you can cash in some of your policies and use the money now, leaving just enough in the kitty to handle any "liquidity" problems that might arise after your death. (See details on life insurance in Chapter 10.)

Make special bequests
If there are special bequests, such as an antique chair or a coin collection, they can be included in your will. You also can state that all other belongings, not specifically named, should go to a specific person or persons—or to a charity.

Leave final instructions
You can also draw up an informal "list of instructions" for your executor or survivors to follow. This can include the distribution of certain items, and it can include instructions for your funeral and burial. The more thought and planning that go into these final instructions, the better off your survivors will be. It can cut out a lot of anguish and reduce the funeral costs. The last thing you want is your spouse, son, daughter, brother, sister, whomever to be "sold" a lot of

expensive funeral trappings you never cared about in the first place.

"There are inexpensive funeral options available," stresses Thomas C. Nelson, senior consumer affairs coordinator for AARP and author of *It's Your Choice: The Practical Guide to Planning a Funeral,* an AARP Book. Nelson points out that "one option worth investigating is a memorial society. It's not necessary to spend thousands of dollars on a funeral. A memorial society can arrange for a low-cost dignified funeral on behalf of the consumer."

If you're interested in joining a not-for-profit memorial society which refers members to cooperating funeral directors to obtain inexpensive but entirely adequate funerals, write for information to: Continental Association of Funeral and Memorial Societies, 1146 19th Street, N.W., Third Floor, Washington, DC 20036.

It's Your Choice gives details on memorial societies and key facts about funeral prices, legal requirements, and options to help both survivors arranging funerals for deceased loved ones and individuals formulating their own personal plans. Checklists and personal planning forms are included.

To order a copy send your check/money order to: AARP Books, 400 South Edward Street, Mount Prospect, IL 60056. Cost is $4.95 plus $1.30 postage and handling charge. AARP members can obtain a copy for $2.20 plus $1.30 by writing their membership number on their orders.

Consider prenuptial agreements

If you are in love for the second time, or the upteenth time, and plan to marry, you might want to consider a prenuptial agreement. This way, you might be able to soothe your children's ruffled feelings if they're suspicious of the "new man" or "new woman" in their parent's life. You can sort out who will get what in case of your death. It's a list of intentions. Actually, any time after your marriage, you can change your will to do anything you want about your estate. The will would override the terms of the prenuptial agreement.

A prenuptial agreement is usually suggested when one of the parties has considerably more wealth than the other. It can also serve as an organized and equitable blueprint for the division of property in case of a divorce later on. The stipulations can't be enforced while you're still married— only after you die or are divorced. Your will or divorce decree has the final say.

Both partners should have a lawyer review any proposed prenuptial agreement. This type of contract isn't for everybody, but you might discuss it privately with an attorney to see if it applies to your situation.

Ready resources

Techniques for Planning a Successful Will. This 19-page booklet is published by The American Heart Association. You can get a free copy from your local chapter. The Association also publishes **Practical Estate Planning Opportunities.**

Now Is the Time to Prepare is a full-length book that serves as a guide for survivors. It's written by Rear Admiral Benjamin Katz (ret.) and can be obtained by mail from the publishers: The Overlook Company, 910 N. Overlook Drive, Alexandria, VA 22305. The book lines up what a survivor needs to know about handling the funeral, insurance claims—everything.

On Being Alone is a guide for widowed persons. It covers many of the emotional adjustments and financial and legal problems that confront a widowed person. You can get a copy by writing: AARP, 1909 K Street, N.W., Washington, DC 20049.

It's Your Choice: The Practical Guide to Planning a Funeral is a very useful AARP Book. See page 177 for details.

Worksheet 7   List of important papers

Check off the important papers held by you or your spouse. If papers are held jointly, indicate under "You" and "Spouse" columns. Write where they are located. (Papers are grouped on the worksheet according to the best, or recommended, location.)

	You	Spouse	Location
Best location: lawyer's office, fireproof box			
Will	_____	_____	_____
Best location: safety deposit box			
Copy of will	_____	_____	_____
Birth certificate	_____	_____	_____
Citizenship papers	_____	_____	_____
Marriage certificates	_____	_____	_____
Adoption papers	_____	_____	_____
Divorce decrees	_____	_____	_____
Name-change papers	_____	_____	_____
Death certificates	_____	_____	_____
Deed(s) to property	_____	_____	_____
List of rents, royalties	_____	_____	_____
Mortgages	_____	_____	_____
Pension and annuity certificates	_____	_____	_____
Title insurance policy	_____	_____	_____
Lists of trusts involving you and family	_____	_____	_____
Titles to autos	_____	_____	_____
Household inventory	_____	_____	_____
Fire insurance policy	_____	_____	_____
Military papers	_____	_____	_____
Certificates of deposit	_____	_____	_____
Stocks and bonds	_____	_____	_____
Patents, copyrights	_____	_____	_____
Important contracts	_____	_____	_____

Worksheet 7 List of important papers

	You	Spouse	Location
Best location: safety deposit box			
IOU's, other debts	___	___	_____
Valuables, jewelry	___	___	_____
Copy of master list	___	___	_____
Addresses of important contact persons	___	___	_____
Best location: fireproof box at home			
List of investments	___	___	_____
Life and homeowners insurance, policies	___	___	_____
List of credit cards and charge accounts	___	___	_____
Family health records	___	___	_____
Key to safety deposit box and names of people with access	___	___	_____
Copies of wills	___	___	_____
Copies of birth certificates	___	___	_____
Leases or contracts	___	___	_____
Licenses, certificates	___	___	_____
Education information	___	___	_____
Pension records	___	___	_____
Copies, receipts for warranties	___	___	_____

Worksheet 7   List of important papers

	You	Spouse	Location
Best location: fireproof box at home			
Funeral instructions	_____	_____	_____
Copy of master list	_____	_____	_____
Copy of important contact persons list	_____	_____	_____
Best location: past years records box			
Bank statements, checks (keep 7 years for IRS)	_____	_____	_____
Paid bills stubs (7 yrs.)	_____	_____	_____
Tax returns (7 yrs.)	_____	_____	_____
Home improvements records (all years)	_____	_____	_____
Best location: active file or box			
Unpaid bills	_____	_____	_____
Bill receipts	_____	_____	_____
Savings passbooks, bank statements	_____	_____	_____
Extra checks	_____	_____	_____
Canceled checks	_____	_____	_____
Tax receipts	_____	_____	_____
Loan payment books	_____	_____	_____
Credit card receipts	_____	_____	_____
Appliance manuals	_____	_____	_____

19
Picking the pros

All through this book we have been mentioning lawyers, accountants, and other professionals involved in the art of financial planning. Ideally, you might line up a "team" of professionals to analyze and advise on specific action to take in your upcoming years. There are some things you can do yourself, but for certain major moves you need the help of an expert.

The trick is to get good, solid advice that fits your needs and is objective—not slanted. If you already have a lawyer, an accountant, or whomever, now is the time to re-evaluate the service you're getting. Will your current professionals fit into your new retirement game plan? Or are they people you hired way back when for a special job and have stuck around because of your inertia or apathy?

For example, you may have gone to an accountant years ago to have your tax return done. This accountant may have continued to do your return year after year. If this professional has done nothing more than your return and hasn't come up with any suggestions or planning sessions in between Aprils, then he or she has not been doing a good job for you. Almost anyone, with a little training, can do a simple tax return. But it takes an energetic, creative professional to do tax *planning* that can save significant amounts of money for people in high tax brackets.

The same thing goes for lawyers. You may have hired

a lawyer—one recommended by your cousin or brother-in-law perhaps—to draw up your will way back when, and that was that. Maybe your will needs redoing now and maybe you need planning for a fairly sizable estate. But this lawyer is bored with your account and/or practicing other types of law that don't pertain to your needs.

Shop for professionals

If your current professionals are humdrum, think about making a change. Seek new professionals the same way you would if you'd never had professional services before. Remember, you're the boss. You're the one who's doing the hiring. Don't be overly impressed by titles and any jargon you might hear. Take some time to arrange interviews with several pros in the field you're investigating. Have your questions lined up. Grade the pros as to honesty, ease of talking, ideas, creativity, and—most important—motivation. Does the person really want your business and want to help? Does he or she seem to have a good game plan?

In general, go about selecting your professional financial and legal team the same way you select your doctor, dentist, and others. Get recommended names from friends. Ask other professionals who they recommend (for example, ask your lawyer about tax accountants, and ask your accountant about lawyers). Usually, top-notch professionals know where to find the best professionals in other fields.

Local universities are also good places for names. A law school or accounting school might provide some referrals. Associations are another good source. They can provide names of local members and indicate the fields of specialization. Finally, you can get names from the phone book Yellow Pages. These are not necessarily the best names, but they're organized by neighborhood and, sometimes, by specialties.

Actively interview these professionals. Usually, they

won't charge a fee for an initial interview, but be sure you
check when you phone for an interview. Select several names
from the list you've written down. Give each person a tryout,
and let each know you're shopping for a professional to help
on a continuing, long-term basis. In a sense, let them bid
for your business. Fee costs are important but should not
completely dominate your choice. Expertise, personality, office location (easy access), and overall enthusiasm to assist
are the things you should look for. These are the generalities.
Now for specifics.

Lawyers

If you have an estate worth $200,000 or more (own a home,
substantial insurance, considerable investments), you're going
to need a lawyer who specializes in estate planning. They
know all the angles. Maybe this lawyer is also good at other
aspects of the law or has partners in the firm who can do
other things well (real estate contracts, tax planning, and
the like). If so, check out these other fields of expertise. Maybe
this one lawyer or law firm will do the trick. This will be
especially true if your lawyer and/or firm has no problem
with suggesting outside specialists when the situation calls
for them.

For example, you come up with a great idea. You think
it should be patented. So, you call your lawyer. The lawyer
is not all that familiar with patent law but is able to refer
you to someone who is good and would fit your needs. If
any special field of law seems to be indicated for a specific
problem you'll encounter, make sure your lawyer or firm
has done a lot of work in this area. Watch out for a conflict-
of-interest situation. For example, don't go to a lawyer recommended by a real estate developer if you're planning on buying
one of the developer's homes. You want someone who is
totally sympathetic to *your* cause, not someone else's.

Interview questions

When you're interviewing lawyers for your final choice, here are the kinds of questions you should be asking, as posed by HALT, a citizen's organization for legal reform:

1. Does the lawyer handle cases like yours on a regular basis, on an occasional basis, or rarely? Actually, you should ask this question over the phone *before* you line up the interview.

2. Will your attorney actually do the work? How much will your attorney do and how much will subordinates do? You're trying to avoid paying higher lawyer's fees for work done by nonlawyers.

3. What is the attorney's billing procedure so far as hourly rates go? Lawyers usually bill by the tenth or quarter of an hour. If a lawyer, for example, charges $75 an hour, a three-minute phone call will cost $7.50 (if billed by the tenth of an hour) or $18.75 (if billed by the quarter hour). The same holds true for office visits and writing letters on your behalf. Get a detailed description of all this and make sure you understand it. Ask about fees and estimates for work to be done, including extra charges that may arise.

4. How long will the work take? What steps have to be taken? Ask for a written timetable if the work to be done will take a fairly long time. The timetable is a must if you've agreed on an hourly fee. Find out the actual calendar time involved and the lawyer's actual *work* during the calendar period.

Fees

There are three basic kinds of lawyers' fees. The most common is the *hourly fee*. It can range from as low as $35 on up to

$150 or more, depending on where you live and what kind of lawyer you're talking to. A good average should be in the $55 to $95 range.

A *contingent fee* is paid only if your case is a winner. The fee is contingent on an award being made by the court in your favor (or a settlement in your favor). These fees can range from 33 percent of the award on up to 60 percent. If the potential recovery is high, the fee percentage is lower and vice versa. As a rule, you don't get into contingent fees unless injury and hardship are involved and you could not have afforded to sue on the normal fee basis.

The *flat fee* is used instead of an hourly fee for certain routine procedures (simple will, probate, uncontested divorce, title search, property transfer). In probate cases, lawyers may charge a fixed percentage of the total amount involved. Check this carefully. You may be much better off with a lawyer who charges by the hour.

Clinics and prepaid services

For certain types of legal needs you might want to try a legal clinic or prepaid legal service—particularly if you don't have a large estate. A clinic in your area may be able to do your routine legal work such as a simple will, uncontested divorce, or letters for a much lower fee than an individual lawyer or law firm would charge.

With prepaid legal services, you pay so much a year for a specified number of office visits. You also are allowed to ask for legal advice over the phone so many times (or an unlimited number of times). Letters on your behalf, court work, or additional office visits are billed on an hourly basis— but at a discount.

You might want to try out a prepaid service for a year to see how it goes. The fees are quite modest.

There are regional and local prepaid services—your local bar association, court clerk, or university law school might have some names. Otherwise, here's the name of a service that is sold on a national basis: Personal Legal Defender Program, P.O. Box 20173, Sacramento, CA 95820. Fees range from $50 a year to $80, depending on the list of services you want. You get a free (simple) will, two half-hour office visits, and discounts on court work and other services as needed.

Accountants

There are two basic types of accountants. CPAs (Certified Public Accountants) are those who have taken a tough CPA exam and have passed it. A CPA is able to represent you in an audit meeting with the Internal Revenue Service.

Then there are the PAs (Public Accountants). These people may have taken all the accounting courses and may have considerable experience, but they have not passed the CPA exam. They, too, can represent you in an IRS audit if they have a power of attorney to act on your behalf or if they're also lawyers or enrolled agents with the IRS. A PA may not be able to represent you if your case moves up into a tax court.

Try to get an accountant who handles individuals, families, and small businesses. You'll get someone who can "think small" and won't be overly bound up in the corporate world.

It goes without saying that your accountant should be an important tax adviser on your team. But your accountant should also provide other services, other answers to your financial planning questions.

Listen to what Leon Nad of Price Waterhouse (national accounting firm) has to say in *Tax Hotline Newsletter:*

"Expect from your accountant: an evaluation of your insurance coverage, the pros and cons of various types of life insurance guidance in your retirement and estate planning, personal financial statements for bank loans or divorce settlements, evaluations of investment advice from other professional services, help with your record keeping for your small business, and help in getting credit."

Nad says your accountant must be objective with advice on investments and insurance and should not recommend any particular company. All you want to hear is the advantage or disadvantage of any particular purchase possibility. Your accountant is doing a good job, Nad says, when: you are kept informed of changes in the tax law, you are periodically asked if there are any changes in the original information you provided, and you are regularly presented tax-planning suggestions. "You can judge a good accountant," Nad says, "by the number of questions he or she asks you. . . . by how much he or she probes to find areas where you can save money."

Fees
An accountant's fees may range from $50 to $100 an hour for specific tasks such as preparing a tax return but may be less for other service. Charges may be less if the accountant is with a small firm rather than with a large, well-known one.

Financial planners
A financial planner is a professional person who can sit down with you, gather a lot of information about your financial situation, and then come up with a list of strategies—a financial game plan.

Unfortunately, good, objective (underline that word) financial planners are not all that easy to find. Some who are quite objective charge percentage fees or hourly fees. Some charge an annual retainer. You get a financial game plan and are charged X percent of your overall investment net worth. For extra visits you are charged Y dollars per hour. Generally, these purely objective planners may be too expensive for the average retired client. They may have to charge thousands of dollars to make a decent living and, therefore, usually limit themselves to a very well-heeled clientele. Ask for an estimate.

Some financial planners go to the opposite extreme. They're selling a particular product such as stocks and bonds, mutual funds, tax shelters, or insurance. They double as financial planners. Sometimes their advice is biased toward the product they're selling because they're hungry for commissions.

Then there are those who hit down the middle. They charge moderate fees and want you to buy any product that's recommended through their firm. Some won't charge any fee at all if a certain amount of investment commissions come to them. Some of the better, well-rounded firms can sell stocks, bonds, tax-sheltered investments, insurance, mutual funds—even real estate. Some also provide legal and accounting services for their clients. Others give you advice, and if another professional such as an accountant or lawyer is needed, they refer you to a specific person they believe will do a good job.

How do you find a good financial planner? In much the same way you find other professionals we've mentioned. Certified Financial Planners (CFPs) have taken prescribed courses on tax law, real estate, investments, and insurance and have passed a stiff examination given by the College for Financial Planning in Denver. A CFP label does not necessarily mean a planner is wise and creative. It does mean that he or she has had to learn a lot about the subjects you're dealing with: wills, trusts, investments, tax shelters, home ownership, and life and health insurance.

You can get names of potential financial planners from a lawyer, accountant, banker, friends, business associates and (in some areas) the phone book Yellow Pages (under "Financial Planners" or "Financial Planning Consultants"). If you have trouble finding names of CFPs, you might be able to get names from: The College For Financial Planning, 9725 E. Hampden Avenue, Denver, CO 80231.

Interview questions

Before you hire a financial planner, ask a lot of questions. Be sure this is the person you want to have suggesting major financial moves in your life. Alexandra Armstrong, a Certified Financial Planner who runs her own successful consulting firm, suggests this list of questions to ask potential planners:

1. How long has the planner been in business? The absolute minimum you'd want is two to three years. The longer the better.

2. What's the planner's professional and educational background? Find out whether the planner's background is primarily in a single area or covers a broad field of planning expertise. If it's primarily insurance, for example, you're likely to get a push toward insurance—which may not suit your needs.

3. What references can the planner provide? Get at least three names of supposedly satisfied clients in situations similar to yours. You might ask the planner for names of other professionals (lawyer, accountant) who can recommend his or her services.

4. Does the planner specialize in a particular type of client? Does he or she have other clients in similar situations as yours? Or does this planner concentrate mostly on, say, owners of small to medium-sized businesses?

5. What size account does the planner usually handle? You may get short shrift if the planner has a lot of millionaire types to care for.

6. How many accounts does the planner handle? If it's several hundred or so, how much attention do you think you'll get?

7. What's the reputation of the planner's company? Is it well known in your financial community? Is the company registered as an investment adviser with the Securities and Exchange Commission?

This should give you a head start in the search for financial planning help. If there isn't a suitable planner in your area, you may do very nicely on your own with some help from an accountant, lawyer, and/or a carefully selected broker.

If a couple is involved, both partners should be involved in interview sessions with prospective professionals. Both should know the broker, lawyer, banker, accountant, financial planner, whomever.

"There are a lot of women," says Marilyn Block, University of Maryland's expert on the problems of older women, "who don't even know what their husband's salary was. . . ." Older women, she says, must understand the financial planning process and must get to know all the professionals involved *"before* their husbands die or divorce them."

With a married couple, then, the planning process should be a partnership. Most financial planners and estate planning lawyers insist on dealing with both husband and wife. Rightly so.

Brokers

A stock and bond broker can be a valuable source of information, even advice, but you must take much care in the selection process. Anyone with little or no training can call himself or herself an "investment advisor." No test is required, no certification, no experience—no nothing. Just because a broker is registered with the Securities and Exchange Commission or some other agency does not mean you're getting any training or competence. Anyone, with the exception of a confirmed crook, can be registered.

A broker with a CFA (Certified Financial Analyst) tag is someone who has been tested and certified as an investment specialist. If your broker has been certified, so much the better. Still, even this doesn't mean he or she is a whiz at selecting securities that will make money.

In his book *Fail-Safe Investing,* financial expert Peter Nagan has this to say about brokers: "Too many are 'rip and readers' whose knowledge goes only as deep as what they grab from the morning wire report from the firm's headquarters. . . . Their records are usually spotty. Last year's most successful and celebrated pickers may bomb the next time out."

Nagan says a broker "who promises little but—after a trial period—does fairly well" is the one you should stick with. The best broker-investor relationship is the one where important information is passed back and forth freely. You outline your goals (income, growth, or a combination of the two) and the broker keeps you informed about special securities or market situations.

Ideally, you should use the broker's comments as part of your overall information gathering plan. Learn about the industry and the particular business you're investing in. Have the broker supply information from the brokerage company's industry specialists (oil, public utilities, and the like). In Chapter 8 we warned about relying too heavily on advice from brokers. You're paddling in dangerous waters when you let a broker "take over" your investments. Listen to the broker's advice and read the analytical reports and eventually choose an investment based on *your* total research.

Brokers will buy shares in mutual funds for you if you don't want to get into the selection process for individual stocks and bonds. But you'll be paying a commission for a load fund. You're usually better off buying into a no-load (no commission) fund yourself. (See Chapter 8 for more on load and no-load mutual funds.)

More and more brokers these days are branching out into the sale of life insurance and annuities, which were once exclusively the realm of insurance agents. If you know what you're doing, you can get these insurance products at a good price from brokers. But check with your insurance company or other companies for a counter offer (with explanations) before you ditch your policies as part of a broker's investment scheme. In some cases, the broker may be biased toward securities' sales and will put you into the cheapest possible life insurance with no stipulated safeguards. The money you "save" by not paying higher premiums for regular life insurance is invested in some stock the broker is touting. The broker gets a commission both ways. This may be just the right combination for you. But, then again, it may not. This is why you should always temper one professional's advice with another's analysis and comment.

Discount brokers

If you belong to an investment club or otherwise do a considerable amount of investment research on your own, the only thing you really need from a broker is the fulfillment of buy and sell orders. In this case, you may be better off with a *discount broker.* These brokerage firms just process orders. They don't give advice, they don't sit and chat, they don't supply analytical reports, and they charge a fraction of what you'd have to pay a full-service broker. Discount brokers advertise in the financial pages of metropolitan newspapers and the *Wall Street Journal.*

Full-service brokers

In general, a big national company such as Merrill Lynch or E. F. Hutton will have lots of services to offer (computerized statements, analytical reports, even seminars). A smaller, local brokerage firm may not have as wide a range of services but may have a keener knowledge of stocks marketed by local companies. Some investors have done very well with carefully selected local stocks. If they're interested, they can usually visit the company they're investing in. On invitation, arranged by the company's public relations department, they get to talk to the management and employees and to see how the product is faring first hand.

Don't just accept the first broker who answers the phone or the first one who is free when you make a personal visit. Talk to the firm's manager. Outline your goals and your needs. Ask the manager to select someone who is seasoned, competent, and compatible. Then give him or her a six-month or twelve-month tryout. If the broker follows your orders and you do fairly well, stretch your tryout to another six months or another year. At any time you think you're not doing well or are not communicating well with your broker, break off the arrangement. Get yourself someone else or be a do-it-yourselfer with a discounter handling the orders.

Rather than calling cold, you might want to get prospective brokers' names from friends and other professionals. Also, ask your broker for references from three or four clients. Call the clients and see how they like the broker's services and advice. Make sure the clients have been with the broker long enough (a year or two) to know how he or she does in an up market—and a down market.

Bankers

A bank can offer a nice base of financial operations for retired people. Larger savings and loans and credit unions offer similar banking services (checking account, money market account, record keeping).

A bank manager can become a good friend and adviser. He or she can give you names of other professionals you might need and will do so with objectivity. If you start a small business at home, a bank loan officer can be helpful by pointing out weak spots in your marketing or production plans. And bank officers can suggest names of other customers who may be able to help you with your business (as suppliers or as eventual customers).

Some of the larger banks have trust departments that may be just the thing for some retired people. A trust department can handle securities and savings accounts for you at your direction, putting in the buy and sell orders, transferring funds, and making sure idle cash is socked away in a high interest money market account. This kind of service is usually called an *agency account.* You pay a fee based on how much money is involved, with minimums set at around $300 to $500 a year. For your money, you get a safe place for your investments and you get excellent monthly statements showing just where you stand (transactions, cash balance, securities balance, profit and loss). At the end of the year, these statements make your tax return work a lot simpler.

Trust departments also have *managed accounts,* where your money is invested for you. Annual fees for this service are generally much higher, in the thousands of dollars. And trust departments don't have very good records for making money for their clients. They're often overly conservative. Some have pooled investment accounts similar to mutual funds, and fees for this service are much lower. But, again, you may be able to do better with a carefully selected no-load (no commission) mutual fund. Ask for the bank investment record to see how it compares with mutual funds.

Sometimes money is left in a bank trust for an heir because the heir doesn't have a clue about finances. The bank trust department handles everything and just mails money out to the heir. At least the survivor's capital is kept safe and sound, free from the ravages of con artists and investment "experts." But anyone with any smarts at all about finances should do better managing his or her own money.

Ready resources

Shopping for a Lawyer. This 30-page booklet is published by HALT, 201 Massachusetts Avenue, N.E., Suite 319, Washington, DC 20002. It gives details on the services of different kinds of lawyers and how to pick a lawyer. It also provides a series of sample contracts for legal services. This booklet and several others on such subjects as real estate law, small claims courts, and probate procedures are sent out to people who donate $15 to HALT for its efforts toward legal reform. A good buy.

Your Retirement Legal Guide is published by AARP, 215 Long Beach Boulevard, Long Beach, CA 90801. It's a free booklet that goes into such things as how to find the right lawyer, questions to ask, estate planning mistakes, and situations that raise a red flag indicating the need for a lawyer.

20
Your financial future

Where do you go from here? By now, you're surfeited with facts, figures, ideas, names, and concepts. You've had a quick course in personal finance, tax planning, and real estate. You've looked into the investment world and now know more than 95 percent of the population. And you've discovered ways to cut some of your major expenses. It's time for action.

The main thing that you may have discovered is the fact that your financial future isn't all that mysterious anymore. You've got a better handle on it. Hopefully, you'll be better able to take charge of your life in retirement and really enjoy the upcoming years.

You've got some goals jotted down. You may not be able to do all you've conjured up, but you'll be able to accomplish a lot more than you may have thought was possible.

You've learned that the priority item on your financial list should be your home. It usually involves your biggest capital expenditures and your biggest operating expenses.

You may have been encouraged to turn your home into a money maker instead of a money eater. By taking in a boarder or fixing up a basement or wing to rent out as an apartment, you may be joining the ranks of the mini-landlords. You'll get extra income and a nice tax break.

Or, you may have decided to sell your home and reap a nice profit. If you're over 55, you may qualify for the generous $125,000 tax exemption on the money you make on your home sale.

A smaller place may cost a lot less, leaving you with a nice piece of cash to invest. And you know more about investing. You've learned not to put your money into anything you really don't understand. Get-rich-quick schemes rarely pay off—except for the promoters.

You've learned that the banks, savings and loans, money market funds, and others are in hot competition for your money. You should be able to earn top money-market interest without too much trouble.

The stock market may be less perplexing for you now. You've learned that it's a lot riskier to venture out on your own, picking individual securities. You're a lot safer picking a mutual fund that has a large diversified portfolio of stocks and/or bonds. And, if you invest your money regularly, like a savings plan, you can "dollar average." When the market goes up, you make a paper profit. Smiles. When the market goes down, you make your next mutual fund purchase at a discount. More smiles. It can take the speculation and anxiety out of investing in securities.

You may have looked over some old insurance policies, at our urging, and discovered a treasure trove of cash values. This money may have been instrumental in paying for a vacation in the sun, a camper, or some other "goal" on your list.

While this book has concentrated on your financial situation, you've also learned that your mind and body must be attended to or "it'll cost ya." Education and exercise can keep your mind and body active and productive.

Perhaps you were intrigued by our coverage of work possibilities. If you've gone back to work part time, you've tapped another source of income. Maybe it's just what you needed to flesh out your burgeoning travel budget.

In the future, during the eighties and nineties, you're going to see many more jobs open up for "retired" people. Our economy in the upcoming years will need more reliable workers. And the biggest growing pool to tap will be the over-60 crowd.

You'll also see increasing incentives offered to older people to continue working, if not full time then part time. By working past 65 and not taking out Social Security benefits, workers will be given extra "bonuses" when they retire. (The eligibility age for full benefits will be gradually raised to age 67 by the year 2024.)

The upshot of all this should be more income for more people in their later years. The more you can earn in wages, the higher your income should be. And you'll be holding off tapping your retirement funds. When you can't work—or don't want to—you should have more funds to make life more interesting and secure.

If one of your goals is more sun, you might be able to combine your urge to work at a part time job with enjoying a better climate area. You'll see the migration trend continue toward the Southwest and Southeast. In his book *Megatrends* (Warner Books), social forecaster John Naisbitt points to the "cities of great opportunity" in this decade and the next: Alburquerque, Austin, Denver, Phoenix, Salt Lake City, San Antonio, San Diego, San Jose, Tampa, and Tucson.

As you can see, these are all fairly large metropolitan areas replete with all the necessary medical backup you'll need. They'll be good places for seeking post-retirement employment, if you desire, and—the clincher—they're all in nice climate zones near resort areas. But be sure to check the cost of living in these areas—some could be considerably more expensive than what you're used to.

These cities, and others like them, will all have their fair share of professionals who can help you if you need help with investments, taxes, and overall financial planning. By now, you'll be able to do a lot of research and background work yourself. But at some stage you may need the help of an accountant, lawyer, financial planner, or broker.

In this book, you've learned how to use the professionals instead of letting them use you. You have a better knowledge of when to call an accountant or lawyer and when to do the task yourself.

You've also learned where to get a lot of free help or low-cost assistance (from associations, books, pamphlets, and government agencies). You'll be able to get more assistance locally from various sources. Your local Area Agency on Aging and senior centers can be clearing houses for information and referrals.

Consumer protection agencies are springing up in county and city governments. You'll be able to talk to lawyers or paralegals about your car warranty, a miscreant mover, a lousy landlord, or whatever.

Over the next five to ten years you'll see the emphasis changing from federal government assistance to local government assistance. You'll see private legal services opening up to offer assistance on all sorts of things from wills down to disputes with drycleaners. And you won't have to pay an arm and a leg to talk to a lawyer.

We hope that by reading this book you have learned that you do have some control over your financial and physical environment. You don't just have to sit there and hope for the best as the bills devour your pension.

Barring any wars or chaotic economic downturns, the future looks bright for people over 60—the fastest growing portion of the population. With luck, more and more people in this group should be able to take care of themselves and be independent longer than has been possible in the past.

With your goals well mapped out, with your income, assets, and liabilities clearly outlined, and with your own acquired financial awareness (and a well-chosen financial planning team of experts to help when you need them), you should be in an excellent position to live better, longer, and know with much more certainty: *What to Do with What You've Got.*

Glossary

adjustable rate mortgage (ARM) A mortgage on which the interest rate over the life of the loan varies according to current market interest averages; monthly payments may fluctuate or a payment schedule may be extended to accommodate interest increase amounts.

annuity An investment sold by insurance companies, brokers, and financial planners and designed primarily to provide guaranteed retirement income. Payment is made to an interest-bearing account, either in regular installments over a period of years or in a lump sum. Monthly payouts of set amounts begin on a certain date (annuitization) and continue for a stipulated period.

appreciation The increase in the value of a capital asset over time; profit.

balloon mortgage A short-term mortgage that calls for several years of equal monthly payments and then a large lump-sum payoff (balloon) at the end.

beneficiary A second person named by a first person on a legal document of some kind to receive benefits—money or property—from an estate, insurance policy, or trust of the first person.

bequest A gift of personal property left to a named person through a will.

bond A debt obligation, or IOU, issued by governmental bodies or by corporations.

broker A professional person who works on a commission basis to handle buy-and-sell transactions for clients.

capital gain or loss Profit or loss from the sale of an asset. Long-term capital gains (on assets held longer than twelve months) are taxed at a lower rate than short-term gains.

cash value The amount of money that has accumulated in a "savings" account connected to a whole life, or straight life, insurance policy.

charitable trust A trust that names a charitable organization as beneficiary of all or part of trust funds or property. In return, the donor receives income and obtains tax benefits.

codocil A properly legally worded addition to a will that is a post-script or that is drawn up at a later time.

collateral Any asset that is pledged by a borrower to a lender to insure repayment of a loan. The lender may seize possession of the collateral if the borrower defaults on the loan.

collectible A tangible object of value that usually is bought in hopes that it will appreciate in value.

commercial paper Any short-term corporate debt obligation.

commission A fee charged by a professional who performs a business transaction on behalf of a client. Usually a percentage of the transaction dollar amount.

commodity futures A speculative investment in which the investor pledges to buy or sell commodities such as precious metals at a certain price on a specific future date.

common stock A form of investment that gives the investor an ownership interest in a corporation.

community property In certain states such as California, all property acquired by either a husband or wife during a marriage is considered to be community property—jointly and equally owned by both.

compound interest Interest that is paid on the accumulated interest plus the original principal in an account.

condominium A housing unit with one or more walls in common with another unit. A condo owner owns the unit and also has an undivided interest in common facilities such as hallways.

continuing care (life care) community A retirement living facility in which residents can lead active lives for as long as they're able, get help when they need it, and receive full-time nursing care if that becomes necessary. Requires a large up-front fee, or endowment, plus monthly fees.

cooperative apartment A housing unit within a building containing other units. A co-op owner owns a share of a certain percentage of the entire property, which gives the owner the right to live in one of the units.

cosigner A person who signs another person's loan agreement and thus becomes equally responsible for the loan in case of default.

credit reporting agency A bureau which operates under government regulations and maintains credit histories of individuals. Located in every major city. Merchants and financial institutions send credit repayment information on individuals to the bureau and in return can obtain reports on persons applying for credit.

---

credit life insurance Insurance that covers the policyholder for the remaining amount of a particular debt outstanding at the policyholder's death.

death benefit The cash amount (usually the face value) of a life insurance policy that is payable on the death of a policyholder to a beneficiary named on the policy.

debenture A type of bond or promissory note backed by the general credit of the issuer and not secured by particular assets.

debit card A charge card that is used like a "plastic check." Issued by some bank holding companies, money market funds, and Mastercard and Visa. Amounts of purchases made with the debit card are deducted the same day from a cardholder's checking or savings account.

debt counseling A service available through nonprofit agencies and businesses. They serve as go-between for debtor and creditors and establish a debt management program to enable debtors to repay bills on a stretched-out payment schedule. Consumer Credit Counseling Services is a nationwide, nonprofit debt counseling agency.

deductible clause The clause in any insurance policy that stipulates the dollar amount that the policyholder agrees to pay on each claim before the insurance company pays anything. Usually, the higher the deductible the lower the premium.

depreciation The decrease in the dollar value of property over time.

disclosure document A document describing a condominium development in complete financial detail.

discount broker A securities or real estate broker who provides limited services at a rate discounted compared to that for full services.

dividend A share of the profits paid to stockholders. Preferred stockholders receive a fixed rate. Common stockholders receive rates reflecting the degree of profit earned.

dollar cost averaging A systematic way of investing a fixed dollar amount at regular intervals in stocks or mutual funds.

electronic fund transfers (EFT) A blanket term used to describe banking transactions such as deposits and withdrawals that can be effected by electronic "pushbutton" activation of computerized operations.

equity conversion A term used to describe several different financing plans primarily for older homeowners, which enable homeowners to use their equity (debt-free value of their property) to finance their continued stay in their homes.

estate taxes Federal and/or state taxes that may have to be paid by inheritors of an estate (the total assets minus liabilities left by a person at death).

estimated tax payments Quarterly payments based on estimated annual income that must be sent to the IRS by taxpayers whose income is not subject to withholding.

executor The person or persons (co-executors) named in a will to administer an estate according to the provisions of the will.

financial planner A professional who analyzes a client's financial position and recommends strategies for improving it.

float The advantage of retaining use of one's money from the time a purchase is charged until a payment check actually clears the bank—which can take several months.

gold bullion coins The most convenient form of gold investment. Issued by several different countries, including the United States, and traded on gold exchanges. Can be bought at coin dealers or through brokers and some banks.

group living An arrangement whereby a group of persons rent or buy a dwelling and share equally in expenses. Sometimes a community sponsors the arrangement and a paid professional supervises the running of the household.

growth stock The common stock of a company with a history of rapid expansion and a forecast of continued increase in earnings.

health maintenance organization (HMO) A membership group which offers all health care services to enrolled members, who pay a monthly fee, or premium.

home sharing An arrangement whereby an older homeowner is matched with a sharer-renter, who shares living expenses and/or chores.

income averaging An IRS-sanctioned way to spread one year's high income over a period of years for income tax purposes.

inflation A rapid rise in prices over a relatively short time, resulting in a decrease in the buying power of currency.

interest rate The amount of money paid by a borrower to a lender for the use of money, expressed as a percentage of the principal amount loaned.

intestate The term for the circumstance of having died without leaving a will.

investment club A way to join with other novice investors and pool small dollar amounts to buy stocks and learn more about the stock market at the same time.

investment company A company that invests in other companies.

IRA An Individual Retirement Account—for employed people up to age 70½ to deposit earned money up to $2,000 yearly and gain tax deferment on the money plus interest accrued.

irrevocable trust A type of living trust (which goes into effect while the trust maker is alive) that cannot be changed or canceled.

life estate agreement A legal arrangement whereby a homeowner donates a home to a qualified charitable organization in exchange for the right to live in the home for the rest of his or her life.

limited partnership A tax-sheltered investment plan in which general partners develop business ventures and invite investors in as limited partners (they do not share in partnership responsibilities or liabilities).

liquidity The ease with which an asset can be converted to cash.

living trust A trust that goes into effect during the trust maker's lifetime. It may be revocable (can be changed or canceled) or irrevocable.

load fund A mutual fund whose shares are sold by representatives who charge a commission on each sale.

market price The latest reported sales price of a security bought and sold on exchanges or over the counter.

maturity The specified date on which full repayment on a security or loan comes due.

money market The financial world's term for the markets where short-term securities of governmental bodies, corporations, and financial institutions are bought and sold.

money market account A type of insured savings account offered by financial institutions in which deposits of a minimum of $2,500 earn money-market interest rates.

money market fund A type of mutual fund which invests only in short-term money market securities. Shareholders buy in at a fixed rate per share and earn fluctuating interest rates.

municipal bonds Debt obligations issued by state and local governments and municipalities. Exempt from federal income taxes.

mutual fund An investment company that sells shares to the general public and invests in securities to earn money for shareholders.

net worth The total dollar value of an individual's owned assets minus liabilities.

no-load fund A mutual fund that sells its shares directly by mail to shareholders and thus avoids having shareholders pay commissions to sales representatives.

NOW Negotiable Order of Withdrawal—a term for a check written on an interest-paying checking account.

over-the-counter Not a location but a term for the market among a network of securities dealers who trade securities not listed on any exchange.

probate The court process whereby a will is established as authentic and the carrying out of the provisions of the will by the executor is supervised.

prospectus A detailed formal description of a mutual fund or security or other investment opportunity.

replacement value For residential insurance purposes, the estimated dollar amount it would cost to rebuild a house in the same place at today's prices, excluding the value of land.

reverse mortgage A financing scheme for older homeowners with paid-up homes to use their equity to remain in their homes. The homeowner borrows from a lending institution an amount equal to 60 to 80 percent of the home value. The institution pays out the loan funds monthly for a certain period. At the end of the loan period, the homeowner has to repay the loan, usually by sale of the home. If the homeowner dies before the end of the loan payment period, the house is sold to satisfy the debt.

revocable trust A type of living trust (which takes effect during the lifetime of the trust maker) that can be canceled or have terms changed.

rollover A *rollover IRA* is a special IRA just to house a lump-sum payment from a pension plan and thus defer payment of taxes. Regular IRA account funds can be moved, or *rolled over,* from one type of investment custodian to another once yearly. A certificate of deposit that matures can be *rolled over* into the same type of certificate for a new term of deposit.

sale leaseback A financing arrangement that enables older homeowners to use their equity to stay in their homes. A buyer purchases the house at a below-market price and assumes ownership costs. A down payment is paid to the seller, and the rest is paid out over a stipulated number of years. At the time of sale, a lease is entered into and the seller becomes a renter.

security A bill, note, bond, stock certificate, which serves as evidence of debt or property.

shared equity A financing arrangement for buying residential real estate in which an investor and homeowner-resident share in all costs as well as in equity in the house.

Social Security tax An income tax that must be paid starting in 1984 by taxpayers whose total annual income (adjusted gross income, money from tax-exempt bonds, and one-half of Social Security benefits) exceeds $25,000 ($32,000 for married couples).

stock A share in the ownership of a company.

stock market An organized system of buying and selling securities, either in particular places called stock exchanges or over the counter, among a network of securities dealers.

supplemental health insurance Any kind of health insurance that will supplement Medicare benefits. A supplemental policy that is specifically advertised to fill most of the gaps in Medicare coverage is called a "Medigap," or "wraparound," policy.

Tax-Aide A program sponsored by AARP in many communities, in which older trained volunteers counsel older taxpayers on tax return questions.

tax deferral A legal postponement of income taxes to a later date. IRA funds, annuities, and some other investments are tax deferred.

tax exemption A legal exclusion of certain investments or properties from income taxes. Municipal bonds are exempt from federal income taxes.

tax shelter An investment that legally offers a way to reduce, avoid, or defer taxes—to "shelter" income from taxes.

testamentary trust A trust established in a will which takes effect upon the death of the will maker (testator).

time deposit Any type of savings account that specifies funds must be kept on account for a certain time in order to earn interest specified. Usually a penalty of a certain number of months of interest is charged for early withdrawal.

trust A legal arrangement whereby the trust maker transfers assets to a second person (the trustee) to be managed according to the terms of the trust for the benefit of a third person (the beneficiary).

variable rate Any interest rate on an investment or loan that is stipulated to vary with future market interest rates.

vested The state of being entitled to receive accrued retirement benefits no matter if one leaves a company.

will A declaration, usually in writing, which provides for the deposition of property after death of the will maker (testator).

yield Dividends or interest paid on an investment expressed as a percentage of the current market price.

Index

Acknowledgments

Tables 3, 4, and 6 on how to read composite stock, mutual fund, and corporate bond quotations in the newspaper incorporate excerpts from quotations in *The Washington Post,* June 18, 1983. Reprinted by permission of the Associated Press.

Selected material in Chapter 2, "Your Goals," quoted and adapted from *Where Do I Go from Here with My Life* by Richard N. Bolles and John C. Crystal. Used with permission of Ten Speed Press, Berkeley, CA 94707. Copyright © 1974 by Richard N. Bolles and John C. Crystal, Crystal Management Services, Inc.

Tish Sommers and Marilyn Block quotes from *Strategies for the Second Half of Life* by Peter Weaver. Copyright © 1980 by Peter Weaver. Used by permission of Franklin Watts, Inc.

Peter Nagan quotes from *Fail-Safe Investing* by Peter Nagan. New York: G. P. Putnam's Sons, 1981, pp. 186–187, 227, 228, 229.

Herbert A. deVries quotes from *Fitness after 50* by Herbert A. deVries and Dianne Hales. Charles Scribner's Sons, 1974, 1982, p. 8.

Table 2, showing middle-income retired persons' budgets in different regions of the country, reprinted from a news release, United States Department of Labor, U.S. Bureau of Labor Statistics, Friday, July 30, 1982.

Table 5, on taxable equivalent yields, based on tables prepared by John Nuveen & Co., Incorporated. Printed by permission.

Quotes from Leon Nad, excerpted from interview in *Tax Hotline* newsletter, Vol 3, No. 2, February 8, 1983. Reprinted by permission, Boardroom, Inc. Copyright © 1983 by Boardroom Reports, Inc.

Worksheet 5, checklist for housing features adapted from "You Like the Home, Does It Like You?" from *Looking Ahead: How to Plan Your Successful Retirement,* p. 26. Copyright © 1979 by Action for Independent Maturity (AIM). Used by permission of Action for Independent Maturity.

Worksheet 6, for comparing costs of staying put or moving, adapted from "Should You Sell or Rent?" from *Looking Ahead: How to Plan Your Successful Retirement,* p. 23. Copyright © 1979 by Action for Independent Maturity (AIM). Used by permission of Action for Independent Maturity.

Scott, Foresman and the American Association of Retired Persons have joined together to create . . .

Timely, vital information tailored to the needs of today's middle-aged and older persons — books that will help you and those you care about live a better life.

AARP BOOKS *Information* *you can count on*

Planning Your Retirement Housing helps you to sort out the many housing opportunities available to retirement-age people. This comprehensive guide will help you to assess your housing goals, explore alternatives, and select the best housing for your situation. $8.95

Policy Wise: The Practical Guide to Insurance Decisions for Older Consumers is an easy-to-understand guide to life, health, home and auto insurance. Written

primarily for older persons, it is must reading for anyone who wants to invest their insurance dollars wisely. $5.95

It's Your Choice: The Practical Guide to Planning a Funeral provides sensitive guidance to both survivors arranging funerals for loved ones, as well as those individuals formulating their own plans. Includes key facts about funeral prices and legal requirements. $4.95

Join AARP today and enjoy valuable benefits!

Join the American Association of Retired Persons, the national organization which helps people like you, age 50 and over, realize their full potential in so many ways! The rewards you'll reap with AARP will be many times greater than your low membership dues. And your membership also includes your spouse!

Your AARP benefits...

- Modern Maturity magazine
- Legislative work benefiting mature persons
- Nonprofit Pharmacy Service
- Quality Group Health Insurance
- Specially priced Motoring Plan
- Community Volunteer Activities
- Hotel & Car Rental Discounts
- Travel Service
- Tax-Aide Program to help with your taxes

☐ one year/$5
☐ three years/$12.50 (saves $2.50)
☐ ten years/$35 (saves $15)
☐ Check or money order enclosed, payable to AARP. DO NOT SEND CASH.
☐ Please bill me.

_____
Name (please print)

_____
Address   Apt.

_____
City

_____
State   Zip
Date of Birth _____mo/_____day/_____year

LYAY

55% of dues is designated for Association publications. Dues outside continental U.S.: $7 one year, $18 three years. Please allow 3 to 6 weeks for receipt of membership kit.

Essential Guide to Wills, Estates, Trusts and Death Taxes is designed to help you plan an estate and compose a will with simple, easily-understood information and level-headed advice. Includes the essentials of estate planning, tables and an index. $12.95

National Continuing Care Directory contains comprehensive information about retirement communities offering continuing care services, including what it costs, where it is available, and what it offers. $13.95

The Over Easy Foot Care Book covers a multitude of topics expertly and understandably, including basic foot care, the relationship between foot health and general health, advice on the treatment of special problems, and the importance of proper shoe selection. $6.95

Name _____

Address _____

City _____ State _____

Zip _____

Send your order today to:

AARP Books
400 South Edward Street
Mount Prospect, IL 60056

Please add $1.30 per order for shipping and handling. All orders must be prepaid.

AARP Books are also available in your local bookstore, distributed by Farrar, Straus and Giroux

NO POSTAGE
NECESSARY
IF MAILED
IN THE
UNITED STATES

BUSINESS REPLY CARD

FIRST CLASS   PERMIT NO. 3132   LONG BEACH, CA

POSTAGE WILL BE PAID BY ADDRESSEE

American Association of Retired Persons
Membership Processing Center
215 Long Beach Boulevard
Long Beach, CA 90801